DYANN ROSS

brokenhearted ness

TOWARDS
LOVE IN
PROFESSIONAL
PRACTICE

DYANN ROSS

brokenhearted ness

TOWARDS LOVE IN PROFESSIONAL PRACTICE

llR

REVOLUTIONARIES

Meanjin, Australia

ISBN 978-0-6459852-1-4

Editor
Wallea Eaglehawk

Copy editors
Sarah Bradbury
Emma Mitchell

Cover art and design by Cat McNicholl
First published in 2023

Revolutionaries
Meanjin, Australia
www.revolutionaries.com.au

CONTENTS

Other works by the author

The Revolutionary Social Worker: The Love Ethic Model
The Revolutionary Social Worker Love Ethic Companion

Acknowledgement

I'd like to formally begin by acknowledging the Gubbi Gubbi People who are the traditional custodians of the lands and waterways where I live on the Sunshine Coast in Queensland, Australia. I gain all my privileges and wellbeing from them and how they've cared for this country for tens of thousands of years. As they continue to care for this country. I wish to stand as an ally with all First Nation People in Australia, in the current political work that they are leading to ensure an independent voice for First Nation People in the Federal Government, through recognition in the Constitution. This is long overdue, and I definitely stand as an ally to ensure this happens.

Mr Thomas Mayo is one of the Indigenous leaders of the yes vote for a change to Australia's constitution. In April, 2023, he wrote a piece in a national newspaper entitled "The right side of history".[1] It was published in the same week that the Federal Leader of the Opposition directed his Liberal Party to vote no. Mayo described how he was brought to tears thinking about how truly terrible it would be for history teachers to have to tell our children and grandchildren in the future that the country did not support the yes vote in the referendum. This is part of what he said:

I hold myself together most of the time, though I am not devoid of feelings. After all, it is predominantly love that keeps me focused, as it is love that moves us to march on the streets in protest against the all-too-regular injustices, the failed policies and harmful laws. It is the love we have for our children that gives us courage to try something new - we have never before had a constitutionally enshrined Voice.[1]

Dedication

I wish to dedicate this book to all people who pivot on the pain of broken-heartedness to express love in the world. From the most private person struggling to survive and love themselves, to everyday people who take care of their family's and community's wellbeing, to the most public of figures who stand up to be counted at critical moments in history. It truly matters to me that you all, we all, keep choosing to love, often against terrible loss, violence and injustice. In so doing we align ourselves with the wisdom and life giving force of Nature. We are one with her in those moments.

This book is in part about the causes of broken-heartedness. It is about the places and situations where love is needed. As such it can often, and sometimes unexpectedly, make comments which can be very upsetting. Please take good care of your heart as you proceed. And be sure to get some support if anything written herein sits heavily in your heart. I do not hereafter provide a specific warning about material.

Lovelessness

WHEN I WAS growing up I didn't feel as though I had a voice. It wasn't that I had a physical or emotional problem that affected my ability to vocalise or speak. I often felt invisible. If I was noticed, it usually meant I was a problem. I was well into adulthood before I realised when something really mattered to me as a child, I rarely spoke up for myself and my needs. In turn, it was also rare that an adult asked me how I was or what I thought about something. I was a little, white, poor girl from the wrong side of town. I lived in a small housing commission house with my seven siblings and parents. It was a very crowded, busy and noisy household. I am sure I contributed to that noise at times. But deep down inside I felt that to speak up for myself was an impossibly hard thing to do. I do remember occasions when, in desperation, I would try to make myself sick so I could stay home from school and be alone in the house with my mother — maybe then I would get the care I craved. For much of my childhood, though, there were little ones not yet at school clamouring for their own attention – and rightly so. As one of the older kids, I found some comfort in helping care for my little brothers and sisters and doing jobs around the house. Maybe, if I was a good girl, I would get noticed and be appreciated. Sometimes I was noticed, but mostly I wasn't. For my mother, the daily household tasks were so all-encompassing that one less child clamouring for attention was a blessed relief. While I didn't tell anyone as a child, I often felt misunderstood and needy. I could not put words to my experiences which were so out of step with images on TV of families being safe and loving. We were nothing like the Brady Bunch. As a child, I did not know the words domestic violence or child neglect. When I was frightened and confused, I was very alone. Being alone in a crowd of family members is an unsettling kind of aloneness. I had no sense of other childrens' home life and if it was the same as mine. I had no words to speak about it or to get support from kids or adults at school.

School might have been a place where I could find my voice but I was shy and didn't push myself forward in class. I soon found a classroom full of other kids my age was no different from home. I remember being almost paralysed with fright in my last year of high school when I was made a prefect, which was a student leadership role. I couldn't believe I had even been noticed and given such an important responsibility. I was part of a group of prefects and one of the tasks was speaking at school assemblies. I would shake so badly. I would be deeply embarrassed and it took all my will to make words come out of my mouth. My handwritten notes saved me. I could focus on reading the thoroughly rehearsed speech and block out all the eyes looking at me. There was also the shame of being poor and not having the right school uniform which was compounded when standing in front of the whole school. I learnt along the way that having no voice was easier to bear than being given a voice and being so terrified.

Bit by bit, I gained a fledgling sense of self-esteem that came from this experience of being a student leader. It was pivotal to how I was able to claim my voice and, with that, my place in the world. I decided I was probably as smart as all the other kids in my graduating class. With this thought, I focused on doing my homework better than I had before. I was usually too tired and, at home, there was no spare place or flat surface to write upon and no quiet time to study. I cleared enough of the kitchen table to fit my books on it and sat in the middle of all the mayhem and comings and goings and studied. In doing so, I claimed, for the first time, my right to do well at school no matter what was happening at home. The gift, which has fortified me ever since, took the form of the first flickers of confidence in writing as a way to have a voice. As I went on to higher education, I literally wrote myself into being a person and into having a future. One assignment at a time.

Decades later, when studying for my doctorate, I discovered how to describe my struggle to find my voice while reading Laurel Richardson's ideas. She explained that we can make and remake ourselves through writing.[1] This idea of writing myself into new realities – to try them on for size – remains influential in how I negotiate new challenges, including writing this book. I haven't been one for journaling, as some people would recommend. Nevertheless, in the context of my current academic position, writing for publication became empowering when I wrote myself and my ideas into the article. Self-storying and studying the self is called autoethnography.[2] This method is not exactly mainstream in academic writing and research. But I find it gives credence to lived experience and emotionality as valid sources of knowledge.[3] Thus, having a career that required me to express myself, to have a voice in written form, was a big part of how I empowered myself. From a terrified prefect speaking at school assemblies in my teens, I became a lecturer at university which gave me plenty of opportunities to speak. It also helped me not be too sensitive about whether the students agreed with me or were even listening.

When I found the idea of voice, it was empowering as it gave me a way of grabbing hold of an abiding experience of unworthiness and unsafety in my childhood. I discovered the idea when I was teaching about anti-oppressive and liberation theories. In this capacity, I found that voice was used in the post-colonial and feminist traditions. A lack of voice signifies the marginalisation of minority status groups. Postcolonialist theories explain the marginalisation for people of colour in colonised countries. Feminism explains womens' oppression in patriarchal countries. Members of these minority status groups lack a politically influential voice and have to find it as part of their respective struggles against racism and sexism.[4]

Aside from the theories in books, in everyday usage, voice is a strange word, and it is far from self-evident what it means. For the moment, I am using it to indicate an ability to verbalise my needs and interests. That I can speak with some confidence. That I will be heard and my needs will be met if possible. This gets complicated quickly as the ability to have a voice sits in relationships with others. Where there is inequality or violence, voice is just one dimension of a person's selfhood that could be under threat. For me, being a girl in a sexist society, being poor and with a working class background, had intersecting, harmful consequences. These minority statuses made my personal lack of voice part of a bigger picture of who is valued and who is listened to. I learnt early on that it wasn't me or my people who were valued or listened to. This line of thinking about voice can be expanded to the current national debate in Australia on whether First Nation People should be given a voice in parliament. Here, voice has a complicated and contested meaning and is central in a political struggle for recognition of First Nation People. It is about their collective ability to have an influence over matters which impact them.[5]

Our childhood and adult life experiences can be deeply shaped by the presence of love, or its absence. My family of origin reflected the dominant norms of the time. In this way, it was a microcosm of the wider inequalities in society. In my family, my mother and father did what they could in impoverished circumstances to care for us. So I certainly believe that care is one component of love. But I've come to realise that other skills and awarenesses are needed for love to be present. Love is also about having a critical understanding of what's going on in the world. This understanding then needs linking to what's happening in the family in terms of fairness and how we treat each other. For example, love is about understanding the impacts if we're a member of a minority status group or family. Minority status people are members of social groups who are unfairly treated by one or more inequalities such as racism, ageism, classism, able-bodiedism and sexism. In my circumstance, the impacts related to our family's lower socio-economic status and the prejudices relating to this. I was constantly shamed around being poor as a child and that can be very harmful. The impoverishment of not having enough money to pay for basic necessities for a big family affected our relationships with each other. Shaming directly led to me not feeling loved. Love is closely dependent on having self-knowledge, knowledge of others and knowledge of relationships and how to build loving relationships. Lack in these relationship areas at home and at school meant lovelessness was a more common feature of growing up for me.

One of the aspects of lovelessness that I grew up with was a strong sense of how unfair it was that my father could be violent. It seemed he could behave however he wanted. There was no one holding him responsible. His mates weren't holding him responsible. Other people in the local community who knew that it was happening were not holding him responsible to act differently. It always perplexed me how it was left to us children and our mother to try and keep our home safe against the odds. This is where my sense of injustice was cultivated. However, I had to bury it because my survival instincts silenced me. I had to be loyal and keep the secret in the family. I realised when there was such an abiding sense of unsafety and injustice, to be loved in that situation would always be compromised. Feeling loved was not going to be possible because it was so unsafe for us children who were basically too frightened to ask for our needs or protect ourselves.

Lack of love had the opposite effect. As a child, I rarely felt safe and was often unable to keep my siblings safe because of the domestic violence we experienced. This had a formative influence on my ideas around love. I would say I did not feel love as a child. I've been seeking to understand love, to give love to others, my whole life as a social worker. It's inspired amazing things and amazing dedication. To be at this time in my life, it is timely to pause and think – what would my childhood look like if my parents had the support and knowledge they needed to be fully loving? What would it look like if they kept not only caring, but really met the needs of myself and my siblings and, as part of this, were willing and able to hear us? Instead, they raised us with the attitude that children should be seen but not heard. This was very much a norm at the time, but it left a gaping hole in my heart. Living with domestic violence that is not declared and addressed, also a norm in my home town, was frightening and heart-breaking.

Lovelessness was about the inability of adults in my life to take responsibility for actions that caused harm. Their caring was undermined by the presence of violence. This failure negatively impacted my ability to have a sense of self-esteem and, with that, a sense of self control (agency). The shame I experienced as a child is a familiar experience for minority status people who are being devalued in some way. For me to be devalued and shamed meant I felt judged by more powerful people to be unworthy or less desirable. For a child, feelings of shame and being unworthy predominantly derive from adultism. Adultism causes feelings of being silenced, not heard and not seen as a child. It is a prejudice so ingrained in society that it is hard to find public spaces where the harm it causes is recognised and debated. Stigma, the causing of shame in people, can have very harmful consequences. I failed to thrive as a child as I was so weighed down with self-doubt, hypervigilance and loneliness. Stigmatising behaviours can take many forms but are usually taken-for-granted messages such as "children should speak only when spoken to" and "she's a girl, what would she know?" These messages are examples of adultism where a child is made to feel less important than an adult in a myriad of ways. Stigma messages and actions are actually forms of discrimination. In turn, discrimination is illegal. Anti-discrimination legislation recognises the harm caused by discrimination of all kinds. Yet it is prevalent and typically not called out and addressed.

Stigma and discrimination are acts of violence and include failures to act to avoid causing stigma and violence against minority status groups. *The Convention on the Rights of the Child* declares that children should grow up in a family environment that is loving, happy and understanding.[6] Like many children who experience domestic violence, I was unfairly treated. I was powerless to protect myself and others in my family. I was denied my right to a safe home. I lost my innocence as a child. I was denied my personhood of being a child with wants, needs, and agency. I was denied some of my basic human rights. It left me broken-hearted.

I had little glimmers of hope for love mattering as a child, little moments of being heard, being seen and not being ignored. It was very fleeting and it didn't only come from within my family. Someone else recognising who I was and encouraging me on my way kept me going for years. There was a teacher in my fourth grade and I remember her saying something to us. It wasn't only to me, but I heard it in a very particular way. She said "You can all grow up to be whatever you want to be, you just need to work toward that happening". And I thought "Oh, I think that's a message for me". It was just a little glimmer of hope that there could be a future for me. That it could be a life without the absolutely depleting, soul destroying effects of living with violence or the fear of violence day by day. For me and untold others, someone somewhere needed to show up for me so many other times as well.

My ideas about lovelessness are strongly influenced by bell hooks who explains that lovelessness at its most simplest means the absence of love.[7] She ties lovelessness to systems of domination and violence.[7] Two examples of such systems that impacted my family are sexism and classism. There was gender bias against the girls and my mother and there was class (socio-economic status) bias against my family. This idea of lovelessness gives us a much broader and less recognised understanding of what the lack of love is about. Lovelessness is caused by violence and injustice in our relationships, homes and workplaces. Indicators of lovelessness are stigmatising ideas and behaviours, including self-stigma. Writers describe self-stigma as internalised oppression, where minority status people take on social messages which devalue them.[8] Whether by our own hands or the actions of others, lovelessness is involved in any use of power that infringes on the autonomy and self-esteem of a person or group. Paulo Freire wrote about it in terms of oppression causing dehumanisation.[9] This is about being made to feel less worthy as a human being. It is not usually caused by an isolated, single negative message or action that has a negative effect. It tends to be caused by recurring social patterns enacted in everyday situations by ordinary people. My family absorbed social messages of shame about being poor and made this shaming part of our family's reality. When the Salvation Army came to our front door to give us a food parcel my mum turned them away. She felt shamed. We had no food in the cupboard. Dad was on strike from his work and had been for weeks. We were in desperate straits but the shaming made it impossible to receive the help. A loving act at our front door was not enough to overcome the harm caused by the stigma of being poor.

The problem with lovelessness

The problem with lovelessness is that it underpins all forms of violence and injustice. Lovelessness creates social situations where violence can breed without the moral compass of love. It serves a social function of controlling undesirable people. It causes a range of experiences in the unloved which, in turn, can cause dehumanisation. That is, lovelessness can make the unloved feel less than human. It can erode a person's sense of wellbeing and can negatively impact their whole personhood. Without love from others, a person can struggle to have self-esteem (self-love) and can't flourish. Some people die because of lack of love. Further, other animals fail to thrive and can die due to a lack of love. Nature loses her capacity to re-new and support life when she is unloved through being excessively exploited and polluted.

Lovelessness underpins denial of voice, agency and rights of minority status groups, such as children in domestic violence situations. In these kinds of situations, there is a failure to provide love, care and safety. There is also a failure to address the harm being caused by the lack of love. The double jeopardy is that the unloved can be blamed for their own suffering. This prejudicial pattern of blaming the victim can hide the broader causes of lovelessness. It can also hide who is responsible for the harm. Lovelessness is not recognised and continues to create the milieu where violence and injustice are possible and socially sanctioned.

Violence

THERE'S NOTHING LIKE growing up in a big family to know how loveless and competitive people can get. There often wasn't enough of the basic necessities, let alone treats. We were kids grabbing the last piece of bread or lolly from the jar. As one of the older ones, I was not trying to be mean to a little brother or sister, but I was bigger and I could boss them around. Looking out for myself, even as a kid, didn't go down too well. It caused lots of upsets between my siblings and I. Multiply this 'looking out for self' behaviour by seven other siblings and it was often a very confusing, chaotic situation. Trying to get my own needs met was seen as being selfish. The boys usually won if it came to a fight. If mum was nearby we would all get a slap and sent outside. Sometimes it would be more than a slap. Sometimes it was a belting. Mum used an actual black belt with buckles on it that could cause welts on bare skin. I was always outraged when I was belted. Innocent or not, even just standing in the wrong place – too close to the incident – we were all blamed. We didn't learn how to resolve our differences and resentments brewed until the next altercation. I am sure I was mean and competitive with my siblings. But sometimes my conscience would kick in and I would share my toys or clothes or make sure my brothers and sisters had enough food. We all would have liked a bit more of everything. We stuck together, in a fashion, as we only had each other. But I did see that some members of the family got more of some things. This unfairness tended to be related to age, the older kids got the new clothes and younger ones got the hand-me-downs. It was also related to gender, the boys got more meat on their plates than the girls. Of course, dad always had a full plate of food. Mum sometimes just picked at the left overs, if there were any. This was just normal in our family. It wasn't talked about as being mean or competitive. But that is what was happening. It often felt like a struggle for survival against my siblings. When we hurt each other, it was very serious. It was compounded by our parents' use of violence against us. It wasn't called violence back then, it was seen as disciplining naughty children. We were all locked into domestic violence by our father. Some of us weren't always kept safe and cared for by our parents. We weren't always able to keep ourselves safe and care for each other. But we did it enough. We all survived. We all continue to look out for each other decades later. But the scars sit heavily with some of us. Heartache and lovelessness were the result of violence that was normalised and woven through our relationships.

Family situations can reflect the prevailing norms of the time, and can be a training ground for workplace violence where workers treat each other badly. Violence between staff can be due to competition for a job or a promotion, for the favours of the boss or for being well liked. When staff are treated unfairly, individually or as a group, it can create a volatile and unsafe environment. When managers act unsafely and unfairly towards subordinate staff, it can create competition for survival, impacts on mental health and impacts on the staffs' ability to do their jobs properly. I have seen this cascading of lovelessness from dominant members of work hierarchies down to lower level staff who then pass the uncaring onto clients who are seeking help. It can become an insidious workplace as staff experience divided loyalties and can wittingly, or naively, side with management against an unfavored workmate. In such situations, good people who are witnessing what is happening can get targeted if they stand up for others.

Throughout my social work career, I have worked in various human service organisations that were complex systems of people, processes and policies. For many years, I did not have a language for it. Without a language for the hurt and harm I witnessed, I felt powerless to do anything about unsafety in my workplaces. Too often, my focus was drawn away from client care in order to survive, or help others survive, in hostile work environments. As a social worker, the places where I tried to help clients were places that needed help themselves. In these kinds of work contexts, it made my job of caring for clients so much harder. Social workers learn about active listening and problem-solving with clients in our professional education. We are taught effective help becomes possible through the quality of the relationship we form with our clients. I did not learn much about the organisational setting of social work. But as a child, I did learn about violence in the family system.

Violence in dominance hierarchies

Growing up we always had a chook pen in the backyard behind the vegetable garden. It was usually quite a big space and the chooks gave us plenty of eggs over the years. I didn't take much notice of them when I'd scurry into the pen to feed them and to collect the eggs. But from time to time, I'd notice one chook often by themselves looking very bedraggled and balding in a patchy kind of way. Sometimes, I'd see other chooks pecking at them and I'd shoo the attacking chooks away. But it didn't seem to stop them. Mostly, though, I enjoyed the chooks and their gentle and friendly ways towards me. Of course the rooster was the biggest and noisiest of them all. He was the most beautiful as well with a plume of coloured tail feathers. I also became aware that some chooks were more likely to get the best morsel of scraps we'd throw over the fence and others always missed out. As a child, I didn't think much about how some chooks got pecked and hurt. They were just doing their own chook thing to my child's way of seeing things. I see now that their chook pen was definitely a closed society of unfree members. The fate of being eventually killed overshadowed the way the chooks treated each other. Their pecking behaviour and unfreedom due to being caged was not a life-threatening issue until a more dominant actor stepped in to catch one to feed the human family.

Being pecked or killed as a chook, being a witness to domestic violence as a child and being a witness to workplace unfairness as a social worker all have one thing in common. Violence. This is about the use of power to harm others. At work, violence can take many forms such as gossiping, bullying, harassment and other microaggressions. It can also include physical assault or threats to harm. The pecking order in the chook yard mirrors the dominance hierarchies of human service organisations. The term 'pecking order' was first coined by Thorleif Schjelderup-Ebbe over one hundred years ago.[1] As a young boy he kept a diary of what he observed in his family's chicken pen. His close observations of chicken behaviour identified a pattern of some chickens being more dominant which manifested as them pecking others. In turn, some chickens were more likely to be subordinated and get pecked. He developed his pecking order theory in his twenties and it has been used to study all types of species in-group behaviour, including human systems.[1] Any good theory helps you make sense of things that previously you may not have had words for. Watching how chooks in my backyard treated each other definitely revealed a pecking order. This understanding helped me make sense of power dynamics in my family and in many workplaces. Unequal relationships are the root cause of using power to hurt others. Older, sick chooks were pecked by younger, healthy chooks. Parents instil fear in their children and silence them by raising them in a situation of domestic violence. Managers and work supervisors control troublesome colleagues by bullying them, or letting others do the bullying, and making the targeted colleagues the problem.

The difficulty I have with the pecking order theory is that it seems to be accepted as inevitable that social relations will organise in a pecking order where some people are dominant over others. I don't think violence is inevitable. But it is endemic in society. This does not make violence morally okay. Hierarchies do not need to involve unfair use of power. However, the inequality in relationships involved in any pecking order can create violence-prone situations. The less powerful in the pecking order are harmed the most. The seeds of injustice planted in my childhood had immediate and ongoing implications for me as a social worker in professional settings.

It certainly instilled in me an abiding scepticism of anyone in authority who tried to micromanage me or in any way treat me or others around me unfairly. This was aided and abetted by reading George Orwell's classic book, *Animal farm*.[2] He depicts, in stark terms, the misery for animals at being at the bottom of the pecking order for humans. Major, the wise old pig, has called the farmyard animals to a meeting in the barn to explain how miserable their lives are. This is directly due to the humans who take from them, don't treat them properly and work them into the ground until they die. The Major continues on explaining how, in fact, there is plenty of food for everyone if the humans didn't steal it from them. Humans are unlike other animals in that they only consume, they don't produce. The answer to their misery, Major says, is to remove humans from the situation, then they can be well fed and free. However, the animals' subsequent revolt against the humans did not fundamentally change the power relationship dynamics of dominance and subordination.

Orwell was warning against authoritarianism in political and social systems. It can take many forms and doesn't always declare itself. One form is the vertical and horizontal violence that can occur in workplaces where there are unequal relationships. Vertical violence refers to the manager's power and control over people lower down the hierarchy. Horizontal violence is power used to create harm between people on the same level of the hierarchy. Human-made organisations are highly sophisticated constructions of direct and indirect power relationships. The relationships are organised according to specialised roles and a hierarchy of responsibilities within a bounded organisational structure. These relationships can range from authoritarian with high levels of bullying and excluding, to democratic and inclusive.

Human service organisations are of particular interest to me as a social worker. The broad purpose of these types of organisations is to be of service to people by providing resources, information and assistance. This might seem like a self-evident statement hardly worth saying. In my experience, many human service workplaces are virtually closed systems of workers acting with a complex mix of divided loyalties, tensions between individual autonomy and the team, and trying to do more with limited resources. In the worst of cases, workplaces are undeclared competitive, conflictual and even vicious environments. When both vertical and horizontal violence is occurring it can be a very unsafe place. But this underbelly reality is not always visible at the mundane level of day to day practice with clients. Iris Young writes about the respectability of professional workplaces which can hide the violences that occur in the name of rationality and care.[3] I would add that workplace violence in the human services is likely to be entrenched, normalised and hidden behind smiling faces and friendly greetings in passageways and tearooms. The smiling face of a colleague can hide the reality of the target being back-stabbed and thus not seen. It is a classic symptom of horizontal violence. It involves gossiping where some staff talk about another person in their absence in derogatory and judgemental ways. For the targeted person, there is no direct evidence of the back-stabbing. Their workmates smile to their faces. Yet, the message is received. They are not favoured and are not included in things that matter. The harm is multi-layered and over time destroys workplace cultures. To be of service to clients, workplace cultures need to be built on trust, goodwill and the ability to cooperate as a team.

Organisational violence in universities

As an adult, I managed to avoid violent personal relationships thanks mainly to having a radar for the smallest warning signs. I was kept alert to the reality of interpersonal violence all the years I practised as a social worker in mental health and community health. Many clients experienced domestic violence and other types of assault. So, it came as an almighty shock to me when I experienced being bullied at work. I remember thinking some time into the misery of it all "Oh my gosh. This is domestic violence. It's at work and by some colleagues but it feels just like what I experienced as a child". Once I made that connection and put the name to it, I knew I was in a dangerous situation. It wasn't something I just had to persist with and hope it would all work out in the end. Bullying in human services workplaces is recognised as a widespread issue. It can include physical assault and abuse and other harmful actions such as targeting or ignoring individuals, spreading negative rumours, excluding them from work conversations and social activities.[4]

The shock was not only that I was mercilessly bullied, it was happening in a university. And not just one university. For the longest time, I kept thinking "No. This can't be happening. This is where we educate future professionals to be kind and caring to people who are unwell or who have been treated unfairly or violently. Why would interpersonal violence need to happen in a university?" Of course, I now would say "Why wouldn't it?" In fact, it makes so much sense that it is precisely because of the nature of universities that it can and does happen.

My naivety as a young social worker protected me from the harsh reality of many workplaces being dangerous. Thompson describes human service organisations as very dangerous places because of the complexity of relationships, processes and tasks.[5] His words held much significance when I read them many years later. Much of what Thompson is describing, though, is hidden from a cursory view, but the effects can be profound. The dangers tend to involve a range of behaviours that reinforce senior staff holding a power-over stance against staff who are considered to be troublesome or undesirable. It took years of being bullied myself at work to deeply grasp what Thompson was talking about. Now looking back over my work life, I can see that, for me, there were two aspects to the danger at work. The first danger was related to being a bystander-cum-advocate in relation to violence. I was a bystander to witnessing, and then an advocate when trying to address, unfair treatment. The unfair treatment came from senior managers and was directed towards other people who were less powerful and lower in the pecking order: clients, students, and other colleagues. In one situation, I had just started a new job as a social science academic. I was so excited as I had been away from the university sector for a few years. It was good to be back. The shine in my eyes soon dimmed, though. I was just getting my bearings and didn't really know the staff group. But, my academic line manager was talking in very unguarded ways with me about a member of staff who they clearly didn't like. I felt very uncomfortable and would try to close down the conversation by changing the topic. I was told the other staff member wore ill fitting clothes and my new boss made disparaging comments about them. The negative comments soon shifted to the line manager not liking the person's values and teaching style. The academic program had a reputation of being anti-oppressive and the person was very conservative. I was told their appointment was not supported by the line manager. I was concerned when it became clear that complaints about the person were being solicited from students by the line manager. In a short space of time, the targeted staff member was being questioned about comments that were seen as discriminatory towards some students. They were also accused of not properly acknowledging the source of materials used in lectures. By this time, I realised it was a concerted attempt to have the person sacked. It was a terrifying matter for me to witness as a new employee. I didn't want to side with behaviour which was already showing as excluding the person from going for coffee breaks and creating a charged environment in the staff group about them. I befriended the besieged person in small ways to try to keep them connected and so they knew someone cared about them. On the very first occasion where I explicitly disagreed with a negative comment about the person by my senior colleague, there was a sudden change. My line manager was very surprised. They inhaled sharply, fixed me with a cold stare and quickly walked away. From that moment on, they no longer confided in me about the targeted person. In fact I became persona-non-grata, effectively, for the rest of my employment at that university. The targeted colleague was investigated and managed out of the workplace.

This brings me to the second danger of organisations which I directly experienced. This danger relates to being the target of bullying where it is not being addressed. I was isolated and alone, trying to protect myself and to resist and survive the violence. I found myself on the wrong side of my various academic managers a few times, well in fact, more often than not. I was usually offside with the manager because I was being treated unfairly. Sometimes it was because I was liked by my colleagues and doing good work. In one work situation, I was seen as a threat to my line manager when other colleagues would come to me for advice and support. The more senior person liked to be friendly with staff and spent a lot of time inviting their closest colleagues for lunch or coffee. Some faculty staff and a few of the sessional tutors would go to a weekly pub night gathering with the line manager. I didn't socialise and avoided creating a clique or getting people to side with me. I had long ago learnt that mixing alcohol and social chats with workplace matters can lead to unfair character assassinations of absent colleagues. I tried to hold respectful relationships with all my colleagues, especially ones who might have different ideas around teaching and social work.

One day, my line manager approached me to say one of the tutors had complained to him about a conflict of interest in my teaching. There was a perception that I was favouring a relative of mine who was in one of my classes. The tutor was a close friend of my line manager and I had been unsure about employing them for this reason. I had given the tutor the task of marking my relative's work. I was aware of the need to avoid a conflict of interest charge and hence I didn't mark family members' assessments. I didn't understand why there was an issue. There was an immediate escalation of the issue to the head of the department who passed it further up the hierarchy. Eventually, still unsatisfied with the investigations that showed no conflict of interest, the tutor put a formal complaint into the highest level of the university. I was subjected to four hours of gruelling examination by an independent consultant. The consultant also interviewed the tutor. From what I could glean, the tutor had an inside story about a lot of my practice. They were not acting without someone feeding them information. This was eventually confirmed by some unguarded comments by the external consultant. A formal report was submitted into the Vice Chancellor's office. In all the months that the investigation went on, my line manager would pass me in the passageway and smile sweetly. I was cleared of any wrongdoing but my reputation was tainted by the accusation. It was a very stressful time and undermined my confidence in my ability to keep safe. I put the bullying down to being a threat to the line manager as they often copied any initiative I took in my publications and research or tried to claim the initiatives for themselves. It felt like I was in an unwelcome competition with them. I was on a lower rung of the pecking order and was not willing to use violence as a way to try to win an unwinnable, undeclared power struggle. There was no love in that professional relationship. It was smothered by the relentless bullying and excluding behaviours.

I've puzzled long and hard about my experiences of being bullied in various academic situations. I wrote an article with a colleague that consolidated, for me, the sense-making that arose from the various deeply perturbing experiences. The article linked abuses of power to the social norm of accepting the rationality and functionality of power over others.[6] Organisations, and in particular universities, exercise managerial authority based on the ideal of reason and with that the high valuing of impartiality and rationality.[3] Of course, ideas are what universities trade in. And certain dominant ideas are, well, dominant. Rationality and intelligence of certain types are highly valued. This, along with the rise of managerialism in universities, has resulted in tighter bureaucratic control of academics. Rational decision-making is regarded as good practice and can hide undeclared biases and emotive, unfair judgements. Young explains that it legitimates hierarchies of authority which can suppress democratic and inclusive practices.[3] In turn, this suppression legitimates that power over people at work actually works. These are taken-for-granted processes that should not be assumed to be innocent of power relations.

Universities, like other complex organisations, function as a dominance hierarchy. A pecking order. Bullying and other microaggressions are not readily recognised in universities but such violences do have a functional value. The microaggressions work by controlling staff who are threats to senior colleagues or who are judged to not fit in with their ideology or management style. There are a few things that are troubling about this kind of violence in dominance hierarchies. One concern is how seemingly rational bureaucratic decisions can be used in an opportunistic way to get rid of troublemakers or people who don't fit with dominant ideas and ways. This might sound like business-as-usual but if you are the person losing your job after being treated unfairly, this can have severe mental health impacts. It can also affect a person's ability to get another job if their reputation is damaged. The impact of being bullied can go on long after the person has left the position.

I worked in various different jobs before returning to a university position. When I decided to apply for a position at another university, I hesitated because I knew someone who worked in the social work program. They were close friends with one of my line managers from more than twenty five years ago. I had been badly bullied by both of them. "Surely", I thought to myself, "there wouldn't still be an issue with how they regard me". I nearly didn't apply but thought I was being paranoid. I put an application in and got offered the new job, accepted it and was in conversation about my workload. The human resources person needed to chat with the current staff to sort out which subjects I could teach. The next thing I know, I get a phone call from the chairperson of the appointment panel. They had to withdraw the offer of the position as their budget had suddenly been revised down. I asked if there was some kind of problem with me. They said, "No. No. Of course not". As it turns out, I knew someone who was doing sessional tutoring at the university. They confessed to me that they were in gossipy kinds of conversations with other academics about my appointment in the tearoom. I was told my ex-colleague made disparaging comments about me from all the years ago when we had worked together. No natural justice was shown to me. The person who was actually gossiping was listened to. There was nothing I could do, or that I wanted to do. It was clearly not going to be a safe place for me to work.

To say the learning I gained from working in universities, albeit from extremely unwelcome circumstances, has been substantial is an understatement. The experiences taught me how to resist the bullying and how to keep focused on my practice. This took all my dedication and energy over a long period of time. It may have not gone on for so long if I had capitulated and acquiesced to dominant ideas. One common theme to the bullying was the more senior person feeling threatened by my interest in fostering an inclusive and democratic workplace. Another theme centred on the senior academic contesting what I regarded as important to teach social work students and how that teaching should happen. In short, ideas got me into quite some trouble. I was either on the bottom of the pecking order or in a subordinate position and trying to use ideas that were not aligned with more senior peoples' ideas. It is such a maddening experience to be surrounded by highly intelligent, motivated and passionate colleagues, and to not be able to speak of the microaggressions and exclusionary behaviour.

Organisational violence in total institutions

I have worked for many years as a mental health social worker. If being rational is a high ideal in universities, it has to be understood to be even more so in the mental health system. What counts as mental illness is typically defined by a lack of rationality. People experiencing psychosis have lost contact with reality and are not considered capable of making rational decisions. They are constructed as being irrational. One of the biggest taboos in society relates to a fear of losing rationality. This fear is especially so if you are a practitioner who is meant to help people who have mental illness. Practitioners are the sane ones. Mental patients are the mad ones. Such is the dominant discourse in mental health workplaces where professional status is highly guarded and professional boundaries equally so. A mental health practitioner with a mental illness is deeply threatening to this pecking order of sanity. The very presence of patients grappling with mental health challenges is also deeply threatening.

I began my social work career at an old hospital in Tasmania, and like many of the mental health hospitals in the 1970s, they were institutions. They had a prison-like feel and look about them. The Royal Derwent Hospital was built by convicts transported from Great Britain in the 1800s. It was a very austere building. It had large walls all around the perimeter guarding the multiple buildings inside the grounds. The walls had barbed wire around the top. For all the world, it looked like a prison inside and people were treated like prisoners. I was a brand new social worker and had never actually been in a mental health facility of any sort. To go into such a devastating, horrific and distressing place and witness so much suffering and so much coercion and control shaped my whole life thereafter. At the time, it certainly left me feeling powerless and overwhelmed. What was so shocking was the way the staff were acting as if it was a normal day, getting on with their jobs. I could hardly breathe in some of the wards where people spent their days shackled in chairs and some were strapped to beds in passageways. Many did not appear to be alive, they had a dead look in their eyes.

From this early experience, I came to understand that staff also become institutionalised. As part of this, they can be traumatised, even brutalised if they are directly being violent toward very vulnerable inpatients. I felt like I escaped when the new deinstitutionalisation policies were implemented. The old institutions came to be seen as dangerous places and governments moved to close them down and provide community-based care. I was given the task of enabling some of the long-term patients to move into the community. This meant I was doing home visits and spared the distress of witnessing what was happening to the inpatients. But I was not spared the witnessing of a different sort of tragedy. The people who became ex-patients were so incapacitated from years, if not decades, of being extremely controlled. Their ability to make the simplest decision was often absent. As many reports have shown since that time, the problem was multi-layered, but, in the main, the community was not resourced to care for people with complex disabilities. Many ex-patients became even more vulnerable to exploitation and lack of care. Thus, I did not really escape witnessing the human tragedy that was unfolding around me.

To understand how violence occurs in a system that is meant to be caring and healing for people with mental illness, it is useful to think of it as a total institution. Goffman coined this term to refer to systems that operate according to their own logics and rules and as a closed circuit of relationships and responsibilities.[7] In other words, mental health systems function to control threats to what counts as rationality and who is thereby valued in society. It does this by medicalising inequality, which involves stigmatising people from minority status groups with diagnoses and treatments, at times against their wishes. Then, with the force of legislation, many less valued people — the insane ones — are controlled by the state.

As a child I had an insider view of one of the most powerful institutions in society – the family. Domestic violence was the force used to control undesirable family members. Hidden under this very impactful experience, there was a prejudice against children. We were not treated as people in our own right with views and interests that were of equal value to those of the adults. As a social worker, I had an insider view of a bigger more powerful total institution – the mental health system. Legal violence and interpersonal violence are the interlinked forces used to control undesirable mental health patients. There continues to be a prejudice against mental health patients that is hidden under these types of violence. They are not treated as people in their own right with views and interests that are of equal value to those of the staff. Violence causes lovelessness. Violence is possible because the targeted people are dehumanised in so far as they are not deemed to be worthy of love. The mental health system is one of the most loveless places I have known. I believe this even though many good, kind people work in these places. Their efforts to be good and kind to the inpatients are swamped by the relentlessness of violence.

Who loves the caregivers?

Mental health practitioners are professional caregivers who have chosen their careers in order to help others. They represent the first layer of responsibility for patient care in the mental health system. I wasn't bullied when working in the mental health sector. But that does not mean I felt safe and respected by management. I do not recall a manager ever enquiring about my wellbeing or showing care towards me. If staff do not look out for each other and care for each other, the workplace culture can be very unsupportive and deteriorate into being uncaring. A prevalence of uncaring relationships can leave the workplace susceptible to unsafety. Thus, staff can feel uncared for by management and simultaneously be grappling with needing to be caring for patients. In providing this care staff bear witness to much suffering and distress. Even in the best of possibilities, workplaces are typically impacted by the stress caused by practitioners witnessing the distress and trauma experienced by patients. There is, therefore, a need to care for practitioners so they can provide the best quality care possible to patients.

Organisational violence is the undeclared, normalised force used to control undesirable staff members. It is sometimes referred to as workplace violence or occupational violence. It creates unsafe workplaces and can undermine respect and care in the staff team. Bystanders witnessing a colleague being bullied can feel powerless and unsafe themselves. Many staff have seen a colleague try to advocate for a targeted peer only to be bullied themselves. I noticed that when practitioners I worked with experienced interpersonal violence and microaggressions in the workplace, it seriously impacted their mental health. In turn, their ability to care for patients was also compromised. When staff are unsafe, their ability to keep colleagues and patients safe is reduced or it takes inordinate amounts of emotional work to resist the harm and keep others safe.

In violence-prone work contexts, it is even more important that practitioners obtain professional supervision to assist them in understanding work issues, complexities and challenges. I often provided supervision to colleagues and obtained it myself outside the workplace. Many staff do not receive professional supervision. They can work in quite isolated situations or amongst a large group of colleagues but are not able to obtain timely advice. The lack of support and not having anyone to listen to your work challenges is a less recognised form of neglect of duty of care to staff by managers. Many practitioners told me over the years how obtaining supervision helped them survive a hostile workplace and pull themselves back from the brink of mental distress and suicide. Sometimes supervision is the only place where a practitioner can speak about unfairness and bullying. When practitioners' work performance or wellbeing is noticed as an issue it can be the case that everyone in the workplace notices. Most onlookers, in turn, do not say anything to the person. It is usually responded to behind closed doors with the line manager in a one-on-one as needed basis. This may not always go so well for the practitioner who can become very isolated. If a practitioner experiences mental health challenges, it is not readily acknowledged and it's been identified as a taboo area in the mental health sector.[8] The taboo centres on the undesirability of 'one of our own' having a mental illness. This is the belief that people without mental illness occupy professional roles to help people with a mental illness. Thus, if a practitioner becomes unwell this is very threatening for other staff, and the system more broadly. I have seen some clinical teams manage staff who are not coping by scapegoating them. Research has shown that practitioners in front line jobs, where there are emergency and life-threatening situations or trauma and loss, are at high risk of health and mental health issues, including vicarious trauma.[9]

The risk for mental health practitioners is well known in the sector. It would suggest that a caring regard would be prioritised for a peer who is experiencing mental ill health. This is not always the case. Organisational violence is not unique to public mental health services as I have shown. It is, though, perhaps more confounding and dispiriting for the impacted individual to be working alongside highly skilled mental health practitioners. That is, practitioners understand how to respond to people grappling with mental ill health. However, they may avoid and otherwise not engage with a colleague about their wellbeing. In the nursing profession, this power dynamic is similar to bullying and is referred to as nurses eating their young.[4] Gillespie and colleagues explain that it is not about being cannibalistic, rather it is about bullying, with evidence that almost one third of all nurses and two thirds of new graduate nurses experience bullying.[4]

From what I have seen, the impact of being bullied at work is a serious form of violence which has a myriad of harmful impacts on individuals. These impacts are due to lovelessness. Love is needed to counter the violence. To be bullied by colleagues, your supervisor or others in the workplace can be heart-breaking. Bullying, and the failure to provide a safe workplace, constitutes unfair, unwelcome and illegal behaviour. It can continue, and not be 'seen' by others, for years. It is an insidious and harmful experience when care, compassion and understanding is needed but not received. Further, instead of receiving care, the worker can be bullied and, perhaps out of fear for the repercussions, be unable to name it. When impacted, an individual's ability to remain productive in their work is inter-linked with being bullied. It can threaten their jobs and financial security. This can be extremely distressing, in part because poor work performance can hide the underlying issues of managers' lack of duty of care and the presence of bullying. Feeling unfairly treated was a common theme of colleagues' stories that I heard during my time in the mental health services. Yet it tended to be muted because people blamed themselves and not the system or the powerful people in that system.

Unfairness is an indicator of violence and includes people in positions of authority failing to take their proper responsibility for staff and their wellbeing. The whole point of hierarchies is to have specialised roles and with this there are different orders of responsibility that accrue to different positions. A line manager of direct practice staff has a higher level of responsibility for their wellbeing than staff on the same level have to each other.

Additionally, all members of the workplace have responsibility for how they act towards others. The example of care and fairness has to be shown by managers to avoid placing subordinate staff in torn loyalties between their boss, their peers and their own survival.

A terrible travesty of justice

Unfortunately, the cost of organisational violence which is condoned by broader societal violence, is borne most by the least powerful. In human service organisations, the least powerful people are clients seeking help or being legally required to receive a service. Throughout my social work career I have been deeply saddened by a common theme in so many clients' lives of not feeling loved, not feeling safe and not encouraged to have a voice as children. I found through the stories people told me that my childhood was often reflected in aspects of their stories. There were common themes, but many of the stories I was told were of a much more severe and traumatising nature than I had experienced. It disturbed me greatly that little children were growing up in households that were violent and lacked love. Further, they would present as adults with issues that compounded this harm and loss. Many clients were grappling with issues such as addictions, domestic violence, sexual assault, workplace bullying, unemployment, poverty and mental illness. There is a terrible travesty of justice hidden in the failure to help people but rather to leave them worse off because of their contact with a human service organisation. People seeking help have already been hurt in some way. To add to this hurt is a form of violence that is condoned in society. It took me many years to recognise that seeking help in a human service setting could compound the harm. The additional harm often took the form of shame in relation to the client's presenting issues. The shaming added another layer of stigma and devaluing of the person.[10] I became complicit in the shaming that was often the cost of seeking help in a society where seeking help is regarded as a sign of weakness. If it was not shame based on a weakness, then it was shame based on the help seeker having a problem or being the problem. Everywhere I looked, there were echoes of my childhood when I felt constantly positioned as either invisible or the problem. My childhood experiences should have made me alert to this hidden cost for clients seeking help. In unsafe workplaces, the complexity of seeking help was more fraught. I could not be sure I was really able to help others when I felt unsupported by my managers. It is challenging to listen deeply and care appropriately for clients when you are not listened to or cared about. Lovelessness was apparent in clients' lives and was endemic in the places they sought help.

A key indicator that lovelessness is occurring is the presence of stigma in a social group's experience. Mental patients are some of the most stigmatised people in society. Followed closely by mental health practitioners, although they have a range of privileges that can lend them some protection. Stigmatised people tend to stigmatise others when they themselves are under threat in some way. This is the way using power through negatively judging another person works. It is the way authoritarian power asserts itself and it is the main way undesirable people and behaviours are controlled. When institutionalised in dominance hierarchies, authoritarian power can be very dangerous because it is not regarded as violence. Hence, the violence does not get addressed.

Labels and diagnoses can become tools of control in the name of care. In this chapter, I refer to people who are in mental health facilities as inpatients or patients. This is a fraught term even as it is in common usage in mental health services. I think the label is part of the dehumanising that can occur for people who already carry the weight of stigma for having a mental illness. I use the term inpatient to keep the focus on this very fact, patient status, and to accentuate the relative powerlessness of a person who is a patient. This is especially so given that many people are under the control of medical authorities as part of the Mental Health Act. No other health condition involves forced treatment against a person's wishes.

A repeating history of lovelessness and violence instead of care

Early in my social work career, there was little public debate and almost no readily accessible information about mental illness. As was the case for many others at the time, Ken Kesey's *One flew over the cuckoo's nest* depicted my worst fears.[11] Kesey's book is one of the most well-known fictitious accounts of a mental health ward. It was further ensconced in the popular imaginary (or, the zeitgeist) by a film by the same name starring Jack Nicholson.[12] The fictional portrayal of the institutionalisation of patients and staff and extreme examples of violence captured many of the public's worst fears, and for some their worst experiences, of mental hospitals. The book was written at a time when there was very little known about what happens behind the walls and doors of places such as the Royal Derwent Hospital and, closer to where I now live in Queensland, the Baillie Henderson Hospital. This still operating facility was built in 1890 and was at one time called Toowoomba Lunatic Asylum. At the height of the total institutional approach to caring for people with mental illness, the book and film were warning beacons to anyone who listened. It graphically showed what needed to change to protect the rights of some of the most powerless and unwell citizens in society.

Pertinent details from Kesey's book are used to bring a focus to some of the most disturbing travesties of patients' rights in the name of care. Echoes of these travesties still reverberate in contemporary mental health care systems. Very little has changed for mental health patients over the last sixty or so years since Kesey's book was published. I've selected details from the perspective of Chief Bromden, the longest inmate on the ward and I've changed the term used by Kesey for ward assistants to 'wardies' to avoid racist connotations. Kesey describes how Bromden spends his days sweeping the floors around the ward. Behind the guise that he is deaf and mute, he notices much of what is happening. Nurse Rachet, sometimes referred to as Big Nurse, rules the ward of all-male patients with extreme control which is often achieved through coercion and violence towards the inmates. Chief Bromden describes Nurse Rachet in visceral, cold, and volatile ways. He explains her authoritarian manner is designed to make patients fit into her regime, which he refers to as "adjusted to surroundings"[11] of the ward. This is perceived to be about total control of the patients.

The phrase "adjusted to surroundings"[11] is not adequate for how patients were treated at the Royal Derwent Hospital in the

1970s. Many people with a lived experience of mental illness can relate to the dehumanisation that occurs as part of such adjustment practices. In 2020, Lucy Barker, an ex-mental patient, told the Royal Commission into Victoria's mental health services that she experienced significant trauma from compulsory treatment over many years.[13] She was restrained to a bed for long periods and "thrown" into a seclusion room or "chucked" into the back of a police vehicle.[13]

As a mental health practitioner, I saw the insidious nature of the seemingly mundane symptoms of adjustments at the ward environment level. The most glaring symptom was the emphasis on staff timetables and routines that patients had to fit into. Kesey describes it as "efficiency controlling the ward like a well serviced watch".[11] I have seen patients waiting hours for someone to approve their leave for the day. Some patients were kept waiting longer because they were seen as trouble-makers. The Nurse Unit Manager's (NUM's) manner and way of interacting with staff and patients was one of the most impactful influences on the ward atmosphere. This became evident when shift changes brought different NUMs and approaches with noticeable changes in the atmosphere.

Many people have multiple admissions to mental health wards where each admission can repeat previous abuses, losses and degradations. Another witness at the Victorian Royal Commission's public hearings, Janet Meagher, describes her long association with the system with dry humour. She tells the Royal Commission that she had many nervous breakdowns and she now expects she is not nervous anymore.[13] There was nothing funny about the experimentation with medications and multiple diagnoses while the staff tried to find a cure-all for her. The iatrogenic effect is evident when she explains how the system of care became unhealthy for her. In short, the system was more of a problem for her than her mental health. She became institutionalised even though it was causing her harm over the years. Janet described some of the mental health staff as monsters such was the lack of care and respect she experienced.[13]

I noticed the other major impact on ward atmosphere was any escalating distress or anger and, more importantly, how it was responded to. Wards that had seclusion rooms always felt more tense and staff were more alert and less relaxed with patients. When the seclusion room was used or threatened, fear hung in the air and made it hard for patients to breathe. In Kesey's book, it became clear early that Chief Bromden had been subjected to repeated inhuman treatment. He describes coming out of a mind fog to find himself in a seclusion room. He doesn't remember if he had breakfast but usually the wardies would have eaten it. Sometimes he was forced to eat tasteless mush. He worried about being out cold from having pills forced down his neck. The staff could do anything to him and he would not know. The wardies acted with impunity while he watched helplessly on a urine-stinking mattress, unable to stop them.

This fictional account resonates with other testimonies at the Victorian Royal Commission. Daniel Bolger spoke about being physically restrained by security guards on admission to a mental health service.[13] He was immediately forcibly taken to a seclusion room. He became very agitated when he woke up some hours later and tried to get the nurses to tell him what was going on. He describes the devastating impact of being unattended by the nurses. He was so distraught and frightened that he blames his first psychotic break on their neglect.[13]

Daniel was not told what his rights were and was not assisted to understand what he could do to avoid being secluded. When first experienced this is deeply terrifying and soul crushing. When it is a recurring experience for so many mental patients, it is difficult to comprehend the harm done. Chief Bromden was a regular customer in seclusion. He recounts, in exact detail, what a typical day on the inpatient ward looks like while still in the seclusion room. The ward activities are so routinised that he knows what is going to happen before it happens – the ward door being unlocked, the doctor arriving to check the residents before they are medicated. Through the day, other arrivals – school teachers on a tour of the ward with the public relations man. Chief Bromden survives, in part due to his veiled disdain and analysis of what is really happening. He scoffs when the public relations man tries to convince the visitors that the bad food, the filth and the good old-fashioned cruelty are long gone. Bromden knows otherwise and sees no evidence of the claimed cheery atmosphere.

Kesey goes on to show examples of old-fashioned cruelty still being used with unsettling accounts of trouble-makers going to the Shock Shop (i.e. electro-convulsive treatment, ECT) or having an installation in their head (i.e. frontal lobotomies).[11] Patients would disappear for days and come back silenced and withdrawn. Disturbing descriptions are given of entering patients' brains through their eye sockets. This is claimed to be a big improvement on button holes in the forehead. There are frequent suggestive scenarios of new admissions being sexually assaulted by the wardies as a matter of course. These disturbing scenes are indicated by the wardies searching for the vaseline on the pretext of making sure the injection goes into the patients' buttocks more easily. Sometimes the scene alludes to Nurse Rachet knowing this is happening.

Research shows that sexual assault of inpatients by staff is a significant issue and can include patients sexually assaulting other patients.[14] A witness in the Victorian Royal Commission spoke of the unrecognised extent of sexual abuse.[13] They reported that almost all the people they knew, who had been in a mental health ward, had said they had been sexually assaulted.[13] The risk of sexual and other forms of assault was not proactively addressed in the mental health facilities where I worked. The wards typically had four or six beds to a room separated by curtains. Bathrooms were not lockable but were usually for single person use only. It was not feasible to monitor all staff and patient interactions and safety could not be assured.

While invasive surgery is no longer permitted on mental patients, it remains part of the popular imaginary. However, the invasive intervention, ECT, continues to be used. This is routine practice even though there is research that shows it can have long term memory impacts, especially for womens' sense of self.[15] The Victorian Royal Commission reported on Julie Dempsey's experience of ECT which occurred against her will.[13] She described severe headaches and confusion where she lost all sense of herself.

There is a strong use of, and sometimes an over-reliance on, medication in the treatment of mental illness. The medication can severely impede the functioning of a patient. This can compound feelings of powerlessness and loss of self control. In the absence of other less restrictive treatment modalities it can be experienced as a continuing form of cruelty. Research that sought mental patients' views on what would reduce the use of seclusion and restraint reported themes of staff needing to be more respectful, to listen and be empathic, and a more patient-centred and improved ward environment.[16] Patients explained the use of restrictive practices undermined trust in staff and increased their resentment. In turn, the control increased their resistance to receiving treatment. Janet Meagher told the Royal Commission that violence breeds violence.[13] She became good at it as part of what she felt she had to do to protect herself against unwanted treatment and abuse.[13] She explained how terrifying it was to have no one listen to you because you were not considered competent.[13]

In the main final report, the Commissioners acknowledged that the evidence before them showed unequivocally that seclusion and restraint had a profound and dehumanising impact on patients with long-lasting after-effects.[13] The Royal Commission created an historical record of state-condoned violence. The witnesses have not been compensated for the harm done to them. The policy-makers, managers and staff responsible for the systemic violence have not lost their jobs or otherwise been held accountable.

Too many good people are complicit with the violence

I was one of these staff who are meant to be a servant to the public, a public servant. That is, being of service to the public and acting in their interests. I was not alone in being complicit with the violence. The fact that so many good people are complicit with the violence is part of what makes it so hard to see it for what it is. Violence in the name of care. I cannot plead ignorance about what was happening. My background in several different mental health services made me aware of the issue of seclusion and restraint. However, it took many years to stand up and be counted at work and in my research and publications on this extreme type of violence. I was an authorised mental health practitioner under the Mental Health Act. This gave me legal authority to be involved in the early stages of invoking the Act in certain emergency situations. In such situations I verbally encouraged, sometimes strongly pressured, the person to come with me to hospital. This was always a fraught action as I was very aware that there was no assurance that they would get their needs met once hospitalised. I also knew I could not protect them from others using force or not treating them with the respect and dignity they have a right to expect. I was not present when police or other emergency responders acted by force to restrain a person and transport them to hospital for assessment against their wishes. I was, though, part of a clinical team who authorised these actions. I was slow to grasp the travesty of justice relating to seclusion. This slowness was partly due to not being directly involved in seclusion events against patients. But I was aware it was happening and it sometimes involved people I was working with in my clinical social work role. So, I am not absolved of responsibility by saying I wasn't directly involved.

In one service, I was part of the management group. This group of senior administrators and clinicians tended to all the governance, staff development and other business involved in running a regional mental health service. In forums we had discussions about adverse events and reviewed the statistics for different parts of the service. The management meetings would bring my attention to the use of force as a standard part of clinical practice that was seen as unavoidable. I had many conversations after the meetings with one of the mental health consumer consultants. This person is employed due to their lived experience of mental illness. He had an advocacy role in the meetings and often made critical comments to the gathered staff. I found supporting his views in the meeting and talking with him afterwards was crucial in developing a more informed and active posture towards addressing matters of violence in the name of care.

My clinical social work positions were predominantly in community settings and, for a short period of time, I was on wards in public hospitals where there were no seclusion rooms. But in one hospital, there was a seclusion room in another mental health ward. Patients I worked with could be taken there. Whenever I went onto that ward, I was very aware of the closed seclusion room door. It was terrifying to think of a person being in there and everyone outside the room acting as if it is a normal day and getting on with their work. Patients on the ward invariably knew of the seclusion room which would have been more terrifying for them. If they asked, they were told that individuals were sometimes secluded due to staff concerns for other patients' safety. Other patients would witness this extremely disturbing intervention to force a patient into the seclusion room. They may have known or chatted with the person. I have not directly witnessed a patient being distressed and the staff acting to have them secluded. I am not sure I would have acted differently if I was directly involved.

The devastating reality for many people subjected to these restrictive practices became a central concern for me when the mental health service took a major step in trying to address the issue. Two mental health nurses gained management approval to implement an international training program on the issue of seclusion and restraint and how to reduce and eliminate it. I had the absolute good fortune to be sharing an open office space with them and several other allied health clinicians. This afforded me the up-close opportunity to hear about their initiative and to lend my direct support to them. As the program was implemented, I heard what was happening in real time with patients being secluded. The two mental health nurses were increasingly called to help resolve the complexity of factors that led to the seclusion. The debriefs behind-the-scenes in our shared office and planning for how to proceed were opportunities to support their leadership. I moved from being a concerned bystander to being an ally of key leaders in the change program. I was subsequently part of a co-authored publication inspired by this initiative. The article drew on research that showed how a range of efforts to enable a trauma-informed system of care can directly contribute to reducing restrictive practices.[17] This was a break-through experience for me because I saw how social workers and other staff could make a contribution to stop this violence even if they were not directly involved in secluding or restraining a person.

As a society, we have to do some deep soul-searching to understand why we aren't, en masse, protesting everyday for the ceasing of these restrictive practices in the name of care. Surely we have checks and balances in the mental health system and its interface with the government that protects vulnerable people from tyrannical treatment? Until recently, I imagined Australia's Mental Health Commission was the place that did things differently to model to the service delivery level how it should look. The Mental Health Commission is a national organisation created by the Federal Government to undertake research into the mental health of Australians, to provide policy direction and to identify best practice approaches. Morton reported in a weekend newspaper that the Commission is under investigation for a range of issues including workplace bullying.[18] Part of the Mental Health Commission's brief is to coordinate the National Mentally Healthy Workplace Alliance. Morton cites one of the interviewed employees who says they cannot enable reform when the workplace behaviours are undermining best practice efforts. No checks or balances here it seems. Though there is always more to a situation than what is reported in the headlines. There are many dedicated, talented staff in every workplace. It can be maddening, though, when senior staff, managers and government officials fail in their responsibilities to maintain safe, respectful workplaces so the dedicated staff can do their jobs.

Behind the headlines – a life not mattering enough

Surely there are checks and accountabilities within the mental health system to stop the repeating history of travesties of justice? A patient's death in care is called an adverse event. It is taken seriously as a procedural review process has to be undertaken and relevant changes made. For practitioners involved, it is also serious and can cause them to experience vicarious trauma and mental health issues. It is too late, though, for the person who has died. Each adverse event that has resulted in death is evidence of a life not mattering enough. A closer look at just one adverse situation is warranted for what is hidden behind the headlines. The media report by Aubusson is typical of a number of reports at the time about the death of a person with mental illness.[19] Miriam Merten was an inpatient at the Lismore Base Hospital's mental health ward. The extreme alarm in the media was understandable. As was the public questioning that something like this could happen. Aubusson referred to video footage which showed two nurses opening a seclusion room door and, without tending to Miriam, walking away.[19] Miriam died shortly after from head injuries due to multiple falls. The nurses were sacked but no senior staff at the facility, or in the higher echelons of the mental health service, took responsibility for the tragedy. The inquiry called by the New South Wales State Government showed system wide issues, including lack of training and support for staff, poor governance and inadequate resources. The inquiry report clearly stated that seclusion and restraint would be eliminated if these matters were addressed.[20] It did not hold anyone accountable for Miriam's death. Since that time, the Royal Commission in Victoria into the state-wide delivery of mental health services, found similar systemic issues. Many of the Royal Commission witnesses put the spotlight in exactly the same place. As did Miriam's daughter who called for the public to be aware of the tyrannies that happen in state care.

Individual failures of responsibility create systems failures of loving care

I have questioned my own failure to act sooner. For the longest time, as a social worker in mental health, I hoped that by doing my job well, it would be enough. For me, advocating for change has taken more than my direct experiences of patients' heartache in how they were being treated. I needed to find a different way of thinking about what was possible. A key influence was Sandra Bloom's writing which shows there is a need to address systems that cause trauma due to the violence embedded in them.[21] She says these systems can destroy the place of sanctuary that people with mental health conditions need to recover. Rather, Bloom explains mental health systems are typically trauma-organised, where hurt people hurt people.[21] I mention Bloom's ideas at this point to share with you one of the most significant *AHA!* moments in my professional career. Bloom explains that violence occurs at points of weakness, power-wise, in the hierarchy of roles and relationships.[21] Thus, when a mental health patient is being secluded, they are the weakest point, the least powerful person. For this to occur, there is a cascading flow of failures of responsibility from the highest, most powerful point in the system.[21] The Chief Psychiatrist of the New South Wales mental health services did not publicly take responsibility for Miriam Merten's death. The role of the Chief Psychiatrist is to uphold the safety and quality of care for people who access the mental health system. Two nurses took responsibility. But according to Bloom's argument, they were just two people in a hierarchy of people in positions of authority above them. What a failure of responsibility looks like can be hard to put into words because no one would deliberately act, or not act, to cause someone's death.

At a legislative and policy level, this type of organisational violence can look like failing people who are secluded by continuing to legitimate seclusion and restraint practices. This occurs even though the relevant policy acknowledges such practices are dangerous. And so on down the line. Each person in a position of authority has an order of responsibility to do their jobs to a superior standard. When anyone falls short of their responsibility, for example, by not upholding a duty of care to someone in seclusion, the consequences can be life threatening. When that practitioner is working in an unsafe work environment, their ability to act safely towards a patient is compromised. They are not alone responsible for an unsafe workplace. They share this responsibility with many others, including the Chief Executive Officer of the mental health service, the local mental health boards, through to the state level role of Chief Psychiatrist. Not to forget the Minister for Health at a state and national level. This way of thinking had two immediate effects for me. The first was that, as a practitioner, I stopped feeling excessive responsibility for what was broken in the mental health system that I couldn't immediately, or on my own, do something about. The second breakthrough was that it crystallised for me just how many ways exist to enable changes in systems of care. It became very clear that there was much I could do, including now when I am no longer in a mental health position.

The problem with organisational violence

All the harms and losses that relate to lovelessness remain factors and are influential in situations of violence. Thus, it is not possible to discern if lovelessness causes violence or if violence causes lovelessness. There is a direct, complex relationship between these two phenomena. Organisational violence is a profoundly concerning type of violence because it can take many forms from reputational harm through to traumatising bullying. Violence can become embedded in the routines of work and relationships, legitimated in policies and perpetuated in practices with clients. In turn, the experience of violence by members of the organisation can be re-framed as the troublesome worker or the difficult client. The bullying and scapegoating of staff and the control and blaming of clients are not seen for the violence involved.

The problem is that the violence continues largely unchecked. The responsible people are not held accountable to ensure safe and respectful workplaces. When staff are the targets of bullying and scapegoating, this constitutes failures to uphold occupational safety legislation as well as professional codes of conduct. When clients are the targets of excessive control and blame, this constitutes failures of duty of care and natural justice and the failure to uphold their human rights. When there are intersecting minority status issues for staff or clients, the harm can be more oppressive. The experiences of staff and clients cannot be compared due to the inequality of power and status. Nevertheless, each can experience dehumanisation arising from being devalued and feeling unsafe. In some client situations, the unsafety is so extreme it intrudes on their autonomy causing a collapse in sense of selfhood. Organisational violence continues to have a functional value. That is, it works. In violent workplaces, the mandate of human service organisations to serve the public becomes corrupted.

An extreme form of organisational violence and failure to serve the public's best interests involves the use of seclusion and restraint against patients in the mental health system. A report to the United Nations Human Rights Council in 2013 claimed government sanctioned medical care that has caused severe harm with an insufficient reason constitutes torture.[22] Torture is explained by the United Nations Special Rapporteur on cruel and inhumane treatment as having no therapeutic justification.[23] The powerlessness of the individual in such situations is a key element of inhumane treatment being regarded as torture. It is regarded as ill-treatment due to the profound levels of powerlessness that tend to be exacerbated by the use of medication (chemical restraint). When coupled with routine daily practices that adjust patients to the ward surroundings, there is a concerning travesty of justice occurring in the name of care.

What is interesting is that the Queensland State Government's Seclusion and Restraint Policy leads with a comment on how dangerous the restrictive practices are and that they should be used as a matter of last resort.[24] Yet, research shows that seclusion is used in some mental health services as a regular occurrence.[25] While less restrictive options are not being actively canvassed by the mental health service, the use of seclusion will continue. There will seem to be no other option. But no other option is being canvassed due to the individualising of the issue and the medicalising of people with a mental health diagnosis.

The person is seen to be the problem, not the system and not the lovelessness underpinning the legal sanctioning of the use of seclusion and restraint.

Eco Injustice

Violence creates justice issues

INJUSTICE REFERS TO unfair treatment of minority status groups and individuals. This unfair treatment usually involves violence or failures by powerful groups and entities to stop violence and harm. Lovelessness is the root cause of injustice, and violence is the way the unloved are controlled and harmed. There are three interconnected ways that injustice is experienced — unfairness towards people, unfairness towards other animals, and unfairness towards Nature.[1] Eco injustice — short for ecological injustice — encapsulates these three ways. The term refers to the mutually reinforcing impacts of injustice within and between people, other animals, and Nature. The chapter focuses on two of the dimensions of eco injustice: injustice related to the natural environment (hereafter Nature or the environment), and injustice related to other animals. This focus recognises that achieving social justice for people is intricately interrelated to justice for Nature and justice for other animals. Justice for Nature will not occur without justice for people, and justice for people will not occur without justice for other animals, especially farmed animals.

My concern with human distress and unfairness has preoccupied me most of my career. Such was the call to try to contribute wherever I might be working. But when I think about the parallel harm caused to Nature, it is so threatening and dis-heartening all at once. Humans are not apart from Nature; we are always in and of Nature and in relationship with her. Nature tends to be objectified and exploited as a commodity to be traded to the highest or most powerful bidder. This objectifying and detracting from Nature's beingness is amplified when the plight of farmed animals is considered. These two types of injustice show in the irrefutable evidence of climate change impacts, as well as the extreme scale of slaughter of farm animals across the planet. Humans as a species are collectively implicated in this deeply concerning unsustainable state of affairs.

In my own backyard

There seems to be no space that exists outside of the system of exploitation and harm being done to Nature. Worrying signs of eco injustice are close to home. A local school in my neighbourhood cut down a small gathering of old trees along the edge of a playground. How shocking for the trees to be cut down without warning after years of being safe and cared for. How were the children prepared for this loss? There were signs everywhere under the remaining trees of roughly built cubby houses, hurriedly put together in class breaks. The shade from trees is a welcome respite from the heat of summer in Queensland. The first time I saw the fallen trees when walking my dogs, their stumps were still intact and I was hoping to see some re-shoots. The next time, though, the small area looked like it had been attacked with a bulldozer in an attempt to remove the stumps which had large roots. The stumps were strewn across the decimated area. Our pathway alongside the trees was no longer possible as it was fenced off. It is a loss too for the birds, insects, snakes, and lizards who live in the space. Is this how children are taught to not mind, to just go play somewhere else, that the trees were in the way?

This little loss joins up with all those other little losses in neighbourhoods, cities, and rural locales. Together, such habitat loss comprises a continuing assault on Nature's ability to hold hills and soils in place, to keep areas cooler, to produce clean air for us to breathe and to provide shelter, and food for other animals. I know millions of people really care about and love trees. I know it could be worse. But it is distressing when the loss of biodiversity is considered, such that every tree matters.[2] Just ask the koalas whose survival as a species is under direct threat due to habitat destruction for new suburbs and highways.[3]

Then a devastating thing happened in my own backyard. Let me begin by introducing someone whom I regarded as a mother to all the other trees nearby. She was the most amazing mango tree – her large textured branches reached high into the sky from a knotted trunk that would take six people with arms outstretched to hug her circumference. Birds sat in her branches to herald the rising sun, stag horns littered her mighty branches, mangoes have fed bush turkeys, doves, and other critters for tens of decades. On one delightful morning, there were five kookaburras sitting in a line along an almost horizontal branch. The cacophony of their laughter was a grand way to start the day. Mother mango tree has provided light and heat shelter to several houses in the neighbourhood. She stood outside the house where I still live for more than 120 years. Back then, the farmhouse was on a pineapple farm, with some mango trees around the edges of the plantation area. Several weeks ago during a heavy rainstorm in the middle of the night, mother mango tree came crashing down. It was the most frightening loud noise that made our place shudder. When I looked out the back door, she was gone. It was desperately shocking. Gone – fallen down the hill out of sight. Thankfully she didn't fall on our house as she would have reached far across the roof. She had been slowly dying due to some fungal infection for many years. But she was still majestic and an important part of the landscape and my world. The north facing hill that was her home for all these years now has just two of the old mango trees left. One of whom was close to mother mango tree and was deeply impacted by the loss. Sister mango had grown over the years to avoid overcrowding her relative and now stands alone on this part of the hill, branches growing at strange angles into a large empty space. I feel great sadness, yet also deep gratitude that mother mango tree was able to fall when she was ready on her own terms. And that she did so without hurting anyone. The demolished boundary fence is now the only sign of her fall.

I have considered mother mango tree one of my closest friends for the ten years I have lived here. Who notices that she is gone now the tree surgeons have turned her into mulch? The loss of the mother mango tree colours the sensibility with which I write this chapter. It gives me a sense of greater urgency to share with you my lifelong journey of connection with, and sometimes disconnection from, Nature. I owe my life and wellbeing to Nature, but I have been slow to act to protect her. There is a deafening silence across the planet as an estimated forty-two million trees are felled by humans each day.[4] The collective impact of humans not listening to Nature is creating a serious threat to our survival.

Nature is speaking. The big miners are not listening

I was born in one of the most isolated yet beautifully wild places in the world. Growing up, I never saw it that way, such was the stigma of Queenstown, Tasmania. No-one from Queenstown ever willingly said they came from Queenstown. In terms of its built environment, it was nothing more than a poor quality shanty town of miners' huts and pubs to service the workers. The tiny town on the southwest edge of Tasmania drew tourists because of its denuded hills in a landscape that was otherwise rich with dense forest. The hills were stripped of all vegetation due to the pollution from the old copper mine. Some years after the mine closed down, the vegetation started to re-grow. However, this caused quite a dilemma for the local authorities as it threatened the tourism industry.

Queenstown borders one of Australia's most important wilderness areas that covers the southwest corner of the island and has World Heritage protection. The Franklin River runs through the area and remains one of the last wild rivers in Australia thanks to a major protest to protect it in the 1970s. My dad was a miner at the local copper mine. He took the job, as farming the land without owning it was no longer financially viable for our young family. Being a toddler at the time, I don't quite recall how shift work and the pub culture for workers affected my family. When I was only three or four, my parents left Queenstown and moved us from one farm to the next where dad did labouring work. My childhood was one of constant moves due to a lack of work and accommodation as the family added up to seven kids. With so many mouths to feed, it was hard for my dad to find a job that paid enough.

In what must have been a survival decision, my parents moved to the small mining town of George Town in northern Tasmania when I was eight. It was in this town several years later that my little sister joined the family. Then we were ten in a small housing commission house with my dad working at the aluminium smelter owned by Comalco just a little way out of town. Comalco was my introduction to the insidious impact of mining and the vulnerability of knowing that it was saving our lives and the lives of many others in the town. As a child, it seemed that my dad was always at work, or we were being 'shushed!' by mum who was on constant edge. She was forever trying to keep us quiet while dad got some sleep after working the night shift. Unfortunately, there was one other place dad frequented and that was the local pub. It was conveniently located on the road he took home. He and his mates would often call in to the pub for what they referred to as 'a few quick beers'. Understandable, after working the extremely hot furnaces all day, where the alumina powder was melted into aluminium metal at ultra high temperatures. It was very dangerous work, and the workers had to rely on each other. Thus strong mateship ties came to compete with family obligations. If dad wasn't home within half an hour of finishing a day shift, we braced for how he would be as each hour passed. I was increasingly fearful that he would come home exhausted and angry and spread his misery around us all.

There was a cost on many levels to being part of the mining town and being reliant on a multinational mining company for our survival. My father developed a very serious cough that filled the house everyday and caused him much discomfort. It sounded as though he was coughing his heart out. He would shower before coming home from work but would still have traces of black soot-like substance on him. This was matched only by the constant need to wash the outside of the house, as it too became blackened with the soot from the smelter. Some of the workers, including my dad, tried to get Comalco to take responsibility for their poor health. He was deemed ineligible to be compensated because he was a smoker. This was my first awareness of the callousness of mining companies when dollars are involved. Black lung disease, or pneumoconiosis, is a recognised industrial health issue, and nowadays it is less prevalent but not entirely absent in Australia and America.[5] It remains life threatening in the other main coal mining country, China, due to poorer workplace safety laws.[6]

He was not the first, and many have followed since who have given up their lives to work in a soul-destroying job to raise their families. A brother, brother-in-law, and currently a nephew work at the aluminium smelter or the adjacent steel smelter owned by Rio Tinto. Another nephew works at a mine site in Queensland. Many families have loved ones or know someone who works in a mine. For most workers the wages are better than they could get anywhere else. The conditions vary but it can be dangerous and extremely hard work, especially in the underground mines. Some employees have high status jobs in mine management, construction, maintenance, and trouble-shooting of equipment failures. Whole towns are structured around and almost totally reliant upon a mine or a number of mines and their upstream processing plants. Santini argues that with as many as 1,000 mines closing in Western Australia over the next two decades, there needs to be consideration given to the surrounding towns and environments.[7] She explains that the towns could be overlooked for due planning to remove the toxic by-products of mining, leaving them carrying the cost from these toxic moonscapes.[7]

George Town has survived over the decades since I lived there. Partly helped by being located close to beaches just north of the centre, some new residential development, and being only thirty minutes from a small capital city. The town and many of its people remain heavily dependent on the two nearby smelters which continue to operate despite being quite old industrial complexes. Many other mining towns do not fare so well.

It never ceases to amaze me that large mining companies persist sometimes with hostile neighbours, changing market conditions, and morph and innovate to maximise profits. The costs are borne by minority status groups as well as the viability of whole towns and communities. From an outsider's view, when I became aware of the new practice of 'fly-in-fly-out' (FIFO) workers, I was doubly troubled. First of all, to preface my concerns, the accepted norm was that many towns across Australia were either built for purpose or became, without choice, mining towns. Nevertheless, these towns were peoples' homes and their life stories were entwined with the town, the mine, and local landscapes. Some towns and localities have been adversely affected and had no say in mining companies switching to the use of FIFO workers. The miners often come from far away cities on the coast. This change in its workforce recruitment killed off the need to support existing and purpose built towns for mine workers and their families. The second troubling aspect is the now well-researched consequences for FIFO workers and their families. FIFO workers do not always fly to their work, and have been reported to be involved in many car accidents in transit to and from their station due to immense fatigue from both travel and work. Family dislocation and stress when the mostly absent or tired workers return home can be other factors as well.[8] Mining companies are less likely to be responsible for their FIFO workers as these aspects of FIFO work take place outside of company grounds. This is especially the case where shift work is involved, which is known to cause or aggravate sleeping, eating, and mental health conditions.[9]

These concerns are some of what makes the issue of environmental degradation – that is the cost of mining and the related human costs caused by mining – so personal and close to home. My early life experiences have led me to be ongoingly interested in everything to do with mining and its impacts on people, towns, and landscapes. As I became aware of other towns and families having similar or worse experiences of adverse impacts, I would reflect again on my hometown. It took me some time nevertheless, to link up my father coming home with traces of black soot on his face with the contamination on the house, with the die back of sections of the bushland surrounding the smelters, with the high levels of asthma and other lung issues in the town. To this day very little is known of the health and other impacts of the smelters on George Town, its people, and other animals. This is no cause for taking comfort that everything is okay.

In my twenties, I moved to the mainland for work. For quite a long period of time while living in the coastal areas of southeast Queensland, I wasn't directly aware of mining operations. I remember the jolt I got when I saw the movie *Erin Brokovich*.[10] Alarm bells rang in my head. There was something terribly familiar with the dramatised account of the actual small town of Hinkley in the USA and the towns I was born and raised in. The film was based on the true story of the effort involved in holding Pacific Gas and Electric legally accountable for drinking water contamination in Hinkley's water supply. The company used hexavalent chromium (chromium 6) a known cancer-causing metal to stop corrosion of its cooling towers. The wastewater from the cooling towers was stored in unlined ponds and the chemical leached into the ground water supplying the town. Despite a compensation settlement by the company in 1996, decades later, the remaining residents have no definitive answers as to the safety or otherwise of their drinking water. Hinkley has become a ghost town as people sold up to the company and moved away, and stigma collapsed property values and stalled the town's growth. The health impacts are inconclusive, but this does little to assuage the fears of the remaining residents. Reporter Steinberg wrote in 2013 that the town of Hinkley as depicted in the movie had no Hollywood ending.[11]

On seeing the movie, and knowing it was based on a true story, I became worried again for Australian mining towns and my hometown where many of my family still lived. My father died suddenly around this time and we only found out then that his body was riddled with cancer, with it mainly located in his lungs. We rarely speak about it as a family but we all know the cancer was caused by working at Comalco all those years. I didn't research what was actually happening in Hinkley when I saw the movie, and only in recent years have sought out information about how the town has fared. Nevertheless, I knew in the early 2000s that this was a story repeating itself across Australia and around the world. By this time, I was living in the southwest of Western Australia and had little knowledge of what was happening in the area in terms of mining. I was raising my daughter in the small university town of Bunbury by the beach. One of the beaches in the bay was frequented by dolphins. A pristine, beautiful family-friendly place. As long as I didn't look at the stock pile of wood chips adjacent to the dolphin beach. It was soon to be a shock to learn that Bunbury Port had a major facility for loading alumina from two refineries just north over by the Darling Ranges.

In 2002, the year after my dad died, the stars aligned, professionally speaking. I became aware of Alcoa World Alumina's local site manager asking the university where I worked if they had some researchers who could help them with a community problem. As a social work academic, I might not have heard of their approach but for the fact that I had joined the university's Regional Sustainability Research Centre which received Alcoa's request. It was a hot potato and no-one else rushed to pick it up. Alcoa had hit the national headlines with some locals from the towns adjacent to the alumina refinery, including a place called Yarloop, raising their concerns of health impacts from air and sound pollution. There was very little information about what Alcoa wanted the university to research, but it seemed to be about their deteriorating public relations with the communities. I had previously done industry research helping develop training packages for employees at a steel smelter and evaluations such as public passenger experiences of a commercial ferry service. Alcoa asked for a brief pitch of what could be offered and a costing for this consultation. I stepped forward and was successful in gaining a major funded research project to address the multi-faceted issues. I remember being quite terrified about what I was getting myself into. I also remember thinking that maybe, for the impacted towns, I could make a contribution that I had not been able to make in George Town. I had lived near an aluminium smelter growing up as I mentioned, but Alcoa made alumina for smelters far away. It was a major industrial complex situated, as I came to learn, on what had been the small rural town of Wagerup. When I say the stars aligned for me with this opportunity, it was definitely a career-shaping experience. It was a key source of learning for me with the stakeholders to find fair and negotiated ways to settle such conflicts. That Alcoa was paying the university seemed appropriate to me – they had caused the problems. Some community people didn't ever quite trust the research team I put together and I can't say I blame them. In the end, Alcoa didn't trust us when they perceived we had sided with the community around some of their grievances. The fact of the matter, though, was that we were on the side of justice and were trying to facilitate the parties at the dialogue table.

Alcoa World Alumina at Wagerup mines bauxite in the Darling Ranges and processes it into alumina powder at their nearby refinery. Alcoa produces hard to grasp amounts of alumina in the order of three million metric tonnes a year and now also ships raw unprocessed bauxite out of their terminal at Bunbury Port. Between Wagerup and the Port, along the inland southwestern highway (which runs parallel to the train tracks) there are small rural towns, including Yarloop and Cockernup. When I became involved with Yarloop, it had a population of 600 people and was an historical town due to it being a major site of the timber industry in years past. It still had a sawmill and in pride of place in the town was a very large, wooden museum holding treasures of the railway era. Beside the museum was a low set wooden, rambling guesthouse where my research team and I stayed a couple of nights a week. There was a local primary school, a hospital, halls, bowling club, police station, pub, a church, small shops, and light industry. There were several streets with quaint little wooden cottages built for the workers in the timber industry, and now proudly owned by newcomers over the recent decades. The town was surrounded by small crop and animal farmlands. Yarloop was experiencing a growth in its northern area with people settling in lifestyle acreages. Unfortunately, while I was there these properties bore the brunt of the subsequent unfolding disaster of the intrusion of Alcoa into the town's life and wellbeing. Alcoa developed a purchase plan to buy these private properties near their refinery which caused unfair treatment and fractured the town. As well, owners of the timber cottages in the old southern part of Yarloop found they could not sell to Alcoa as there was not enough value in their asset to buy elsewhere. Many felt trapped, others felt forced to leave. We talked with many of the original residents and came to deeply appreciate their powerlessness and grievances about how Alcoa was destroying their town, health and their property values.

I was given a briefing by Alcoa about what they expected and as you might guess, they portrayed themselves as the victim being held to ransom by 'red necks' in the community. Well,

I have lived in towns with so-called rednecks, referring to hot headed, loud mouthed (usually) men who work in mines and other labouring jobs. One thing I knew was that in all their bluster there was nearly always some truth to be found. I explained to Alcoa that the research would endeavour to build a dialogue between the local communities and Alcoa to problem-solve the issues. The aim was to thereby avoid media reports that were damaging Alcoa's reputation. Personnel I worked with at Alcoa were initially adamant that their workers had no problem with them, it was just those local residents stirring up trouble. We started with a meeting of senior Alcoa staff and managers and workers from their refinery and mine site. It was clear at the meeting that many of the workers, especially those who lived in Yarloop, were concerned about pollution impacts on their families, town, and properties. One worker, who would become a long term activist and community leader, told Alcoa they should come out from behind the dollar signs and show their face to the people. Some workers raised the contentious issue of experiencing multiple chemical sensitivities and other health issues due to where they worked in the refinery. It was an active issue with the union at that time and workers were eventually compensated. But it was the perceived slowness to respond by Alcoa that led to increasing alarm as workers talked about their health issues in their communities.

After this first meeting with our research team, Alcoa was placed in a position where they had to allow a fuller picture to emerge of how locals were being impacted. What followed was nearly two years of research that was action-oriented and participatory between Alcoa at Wagerup and Yarloop and other local residents. Weekly public meetings were held with Alcoa and community members to discuss and try to problem-solve the many inter-related concerns of the townspeople. There were several active resident action groups and a Medical Practitioners' Forum working on the health and pollution concerns. We came alongside these important groups and tended to focus on Alcoa's unfair land management plan, which set the rules for which properties they would buy with an added amount as a resettlement payment. This became a major de-stabilising practice as many people sold to Alcoa and left, leaving big gaps in sporting teams, social clubs, and other community activities. Alcoa was wanting to establish a secure exclusive economic zone around their refinery in the absence of a government gazetted buffer. Alcoa would not accept that they were offering to buy properties because of the health issues that were now more or less recognised as spread throughout the locality. Health issues such as nose bleeds, headaches, respiratory illness, and chemical sensitivity were exacerbated when emissions from the refinery covered the nearby towns. In 2004, the Western Australian Government held a parliamentary inquiry into the unfolding disaster.[12] By this time the town population had changed dramatically. The school, police station, and hospital had all closed as the government was concerned for its staff, not that they openly declared this was the reason for the closures.

I've written about this research over the years and perhaps the most important publication was with my colleague, Martin Brueckner. The book is called *Under corporate skies: A struggle between people, place and profit*.[13] When it was published, Alcoa was on the public record as saying it was a pack of lies. It included confidential interviews with some Alcoa managers, one of whom admitted that Alcoa had made a big mistake by not listening to the people. They said that Alcoa had thrown money at improvements to the refinery, without admitting liability. According to many local people, it has continued to fail in its corporate social responsibility. I remember when we first went to Yarloop, one of Alcoa's senior medical officers from their homebase in the American city of Pittsburgh, visited Alcoa at Wagerup. He said on the public record that Alcoa has a problem and they need to fix it.

As I want to focus on the environment and my experiences with the town from this perspective, I won't further describe what we did, what happened, and how the people of Yarloop and surrounding towns are faring today. It was clear from the outset that the townspeoples' livelihoods were intricately linked to the harm being done to the natural environment. When I first went to Yarloop, the concerns expressed by the people I talked with related to organic farmers being very worried about losing their organic status as they feared air pollution would damage their small crops.[14] Other farmers were worried about the health of their cows and other animals. The concerns were typically refuted by Alcoa, who would rush to say their small herd of cows around the refinery was healthy.

It needs to be recognised that when the local residents and farmers referred to refinery emissions these emissions are known to contain dangerous chemicals as a by-product of the production of alumina. The Alcoa operation involves the use of highly toxic chemicals, including caustic liquor which can become airborne mist, asbestos, and mineral fibres in the thermal insulation, lead paint in the steel structure and crystalline silica refractories used in the calciners. Alcoa has always maintained that the levels of these chemicals in refinery emissions are within international safety guidelines. The local communities have contested this ongoingly and were not appeased, especially when the State Government relied on Alcoa's records of emissions quality from their operations. This seemed nonsensical to me and I would sit in meetings where the concerned residents would challenge the Government and Alcoa about the lack of independent air sampling and monitoring. It did not matter how many times this issue was raised and by whom, there was no change until locals developed an alternative method of keeping a record of the pollution. In 2006, Community Alliance for Positive Solutions (CAPS), a community-based activist group, organised independent air sampling and testing paid for by private citizens.[15] The results were significant and subsequently the State Government assumed this responsibility.

There are two sources of contamination of the environment, further to noise pollution that is not contained within the industrial complex. Namely, the most contentious equipment in the refinery, the liquor burner, and on land adjacent to the refinery, the mud lakes. In 1996, Alcoa commissioned a liquor burner on their Wagerup site. It was installed to improve the quality and quantity of the alumina, but came to be seen as a major source of the pollution issues in the surrounding communities. The liquor burner was very controversial as it released volatile organic compounds (VOCs) which are known to be hazardous to health. As Martin and I wrote in *Under corporate skies*, it was known by Alcoa that the liquor burner had potential health impacts but they proceeded anyway. In fact, a report we sourced showed that Alcoa sought advice on how to respond if there were complaints.[13] From that time, the complaints by residents increased and Alcoa responded with denials and avoidance. We recommended to Alcoa that they shut down the liquor burner as an act of goodwill to the impacted communities. They declined, saying it would be too costly for them to do that.

The second source of contamination is a particularly troubling example of polluted water that is visible to the public on the approach to Alcoa's refinery at Wagerup. The CAPS website has a video which shows the concerning visual images of what Alcoa calls 'mud lakes'.[16] The term mud lakes is a misleading name to refer to an area that covered 1500 acres (607 ha) to accommodate five million metric tonnes per annum of the toxic waste from the refinery operations. Wastewater is fed from the refinery into the mud lakes. The locals believed this source of pollution involved an unknown amount of leaching from the plastic lining of the ponds. The site manager admitted to me that the mud lakes were a major concern for her management team. I became personally aware of the serious threat posed by these wastelands, which cover what was once prime agricultural land, when one of my research colleagues had extreme difficulty breathing one day when we were at Yarloop. Air-borne red 'dust' from the insufficiently watered down mud lakes covered the town and impacted many peoples' breathing and health. Alcoa referred to it as a 'dust excursion' which would be funny if it wasn't so seriously awful. To call toxic waste dust, and to refer to it as going on an excursion, is to underplay the health and other risks involved for anyone and anything in its path. The locals made a joke about it but it wasn't a happy joke. We subsequently had to provide an account of the experience to the State Government who fined Alcoa for the breach of its refinery footprint.

In 2016, a devastating bushfire started in the hills to the east of the Wagerup refinery. It spread at lightning speed and demolished almost all of Yarloop. Two people died and the old museum, guesthouse, hospital, pub, town hall, a shop, and its attached dwelling, and many dwellings (in the order of 160) were destroyed. The museum was flattened and all the historical records and train engines made of steel were destroyed. Behind the museum there was a narrow winding road with tiny single-room wooden cottages lining its edges. It was called Happy Valley. Nothing survived in Happy Valley. The flora and fauna was also heavily impacted In the local area and many farmers lost infrastructure, farm animals, pets, crops, and fruit trees. I flew to Western Australia and went straight to the town a couple of days later. The town was closed for what became several months due to fears about the asbestos in many of the destroyed houses. My long term colleagues were shattered as they showed me around their beloved town. The scale of the loss for such a small town was almost total. One of my colleagues and his partner had lost their house and my other colleague's house narrowly escaped but the surrounding bushland was blackened. His mother's home that had been sold to Alcoa was destroyed. The old letter box at the front gate showed the ferocity of the fire – it was crumpled and black. Another colleague almost lost his life fighting to save his home and two of Alcoa's properties. One of the entry roads to the town from the southwest highway had tall stands of gum trees lining both sides of the road. A truly majestic sight. All badly burned, as were the highly valued wetlands and bush surrounding the eastern side of Yarloop.

You might be thinking that this is very sad but not that strange for Australia. But there is a more troubling dimension to this tragedy that reflected the long term, unequal struggle by Yarloop for protection. Its residents wanted the Government to protect them from the impact of Alcoa Wagerup. However, the Government was also fostering the mining company to expand, still without a government gazetted buffer zone. Some of the residents who were home when the fire hit, later provided evidence to a parliamentary inquiry that no warning was given to the townspeople; that the local fire brigade was told to bypass Yarloop and go directly to the refinery; that there was no water left for locals; and that no help was given until it was too late.[17] The media showed the Premier of Western Australia saying a cloud now hung over Yarloop. There was no commitment to help the town rebuild. Alcoa at Wagerup made no public announcement of concern for Yarloop in the days after the fire. Locals were outraged when they learnt that all the fire response resources were ordered to go to Alcoa as there were grave fears of the fire breaching the refinery perimeters. Some of the Alcoa workers later told the media that they were ordered to return to work to help protect the refinery while their own homes and families were at risk.

Martin Brueckner and I helped CAPS put together a statement about the troubling political context in which the fire occurred. The chairperson for the inquiry said it was beyond the scope of the terms set for the inquiry to consider the historical and political issues. But he was willing to read the statement and be aware of it. The inquiry found the government had not responded adequately to the fire disaster.[17] But this left a number of questions unaddressed. How could it be that there was no regional fire and other disasters management plan, given the presence of a major industrial complex in close proximity to towns and homes? How was it that the water was prioritised for saving Alcoa while Yarloop was literally left to burn? How is it that the Premier could not commit to rebuilding the town? My CAPS colleagues said they were not surprised and said it has always been the case that Alcoa is more advantaged no matter what happens and Yarloop is always worse off. After the fire, Alcoa no longer needed to buy houses, and if they did the value had plummeted. The properties they had previously purchased were destroyed, which saved Alcoa what could have been a long and contentious demolition process.

To this day, some twenty years after I began my involvement with Yarloop, I hold an abiding interest in the local activists' work. They are still trying to hold the company and the State Government of Western Australia accountable for the many impacts of the mining operations. CAPS provides independent research to challenge the conditions of Alcoa's licence to operate, and expert advice to various departments of the State Government. CAPS, in collaboration with several government and university experts, is exploring how to influence a revision of the State Agreement with Alcoa. The Act allows the multinational mining company to continue removing jarrah trees from its mining lease at 100 times the original expected twenty five acres a year. The Agreement is due to be renewed in 2024 for another twenty-one years with its plans only requiring the signature of the Minister for Industry, without the advice of Ministers responsible for water, the environment, and tourism. As Milne explains, the Act has meant Alcoa has not been accountable to the public for 60 years.[18]

Further to my own experiences with mining, I was strongly influenced by Rachel Carson's seminal book, *Silent spring*.[19] I wasn't an avid reader growing up, as books were hard to come by in my home. We had an expensive set of encyclopaedias that were purchased to support our education. It was my mum's one claim to something of status. The bookshelf packed with these tombs of wisdom had pride of place near the front door for all to see. But they were not exactly the kind of book to take to bed with you for a good read. Oh, and my big sister would buy Archie comics and dad had cowboy books – doubly not interesting to me. So it feels like I have spent a good portion of my adult life catching up with important books long after they hit the public consciousness. This was the case with Carson's book. I can't recall how it found its way to my hands and I suspect I didn't read it in its entirety. But I got the message, loud and clear. I was devastated. So began my education about the troubling impact of human-made chemicals on Nature, including humans and other animals. At the time it made me re-assess my early life on dairy and small crop farms. Strange looking large metal containers in the storage sheds always seemed out of place with the gardening tools and tractors. I didn't see my dad using sprays but these containers were filled with DDT (Dichlorodiphenyltrichloroethane) and other types of insecticides. He did not use protective clothing as many farmers do nowadays. In the 1950s and 1960s, the dangers of the pesticides were not commonly known or accepted by farmers.

Carson's book provides a timely warning of violences committed against Nature and all beings through an intricate ecological connectivity. While written in 1962, her book is disturbingly on point for many of the environmental issues, including climate change, some 60 years later. When I became aware of the Alcoa research opportunity in the early 2000s,

I already had a lived experience of being a mining town and farming daughter. Additionally, because of Carson's book, I had a beginning appreciation of how toxic chemicals can disperse through the life chain and affect everything. I also had a sense that it was difficult to trace to the source where contamination might come from and to hold industry responsible for harm done.

In my own defence, I am aware as I write this, that some of you might well be wondering how it was that I was so slow to be alert to issues of environmental exploitation and degradation. I wonder about it myself. My career as a social worker certainly has meant that I was tuned into what happens to people. Social work has this dictum that it is about 'the person-in-environment'. When I first heard that phrase I thought it actually meant the environment as in Nature. But in social work it means the person's situation, the person in their context, and needing to be aware of the various factors affecting their wellbeing. As a profession, social work continues to place people before and often apart from the natural environment and other animals. This was my limited thinking and valuing as well for many years. Even now my teaching about mining and its impacts is unusual and not part of the mainstream social work curriculum at university.

In the chapter entitled *A fable for tomorrow*, Carson writes about the use of pesticides in what became recognised internationally as a major tipping point in the health and sustainability of Nature.[19] She describes the eerie silence as flocks of birds die, children become suddenly sick and many people die from unknown sources.[19] House roofs are covered in powdery dust but it was not snow. There was no war or anything strange that had taken place. The people had done it to themselves by poisoning their lands and homes.[19]

In returning to Carson's book this year, I was shocked to read this allegory after my long-standing involvement with the Yarloop town-peoples' conflict with Alcoa World Alumina. This is no allegory. So many of her points reflect the experiences of the town, right down to the white powder on houses – in Yarloop's case, from uncovered passing trains which were transporting alumina to the port at Bunbury. It is profoundly disturbing, but not surprising, that at this time on the planet, pre-eminent scientists, environmental advocates, and informed citizens know in their hearts the awful truth. What Al Gore called an inconvenient truth.[20] Carson warned decades earlier that the nature of the threat escalated with the use of dangerous pesticides on crops.[19] She explains that the chain of events that follow on from its use causes a type of pollution that permeates all aspects of life, which is largely irreversible.[19] Her book details the pervasive and intricate spread and impacts of the chemicals which act in a similar way to radiation. A little later, she writes that the dangerousness of the chemicals used so extensively might be better termed biocides, not insecticides.[19]

Social work is far from the forefront of environmental activism. Boetto challenges other social workers to recognise that humans have collectively acted as a force with geological impacts.[21] That really hit home for me when I read it. Science has now been able to substantiate that in recent times human-made buildings, infrastructure, and development now outweigh the productivity and biomass of Nature.[22] First Nation People and environmental activist groups around the world have been warning of environmental catastrophes, loss of biodiversity and impacts of climate change. The warnings are so dire but continue to be silenced or not heeded by the elites in business and governments. The intersectionality of issues and devastatingly serious consequences are referred to as wicked problems. Concerningly, many activists risk and lose their lives in their efforts to protect their places and livelihoods from unsustainable development. Global Witness reports that for decades an estimated three people are killed every week trying to defend their homelands.[23] It is definitely dangerous to challenge the vested interests who gain disproportionately from environmental degradation. Vandana Shiva argues that this violence makes little sense when the activists are all that stands in the way of the planet's sixth mass extinction.[23] It is no longer only a matter of morality but rather a matter of human and other species' survival.

Meanwhile, in a mainstream newspaper on the 28th January, 2023, it is reported that the Federal Government's estimated budget deficit for the coming year has been slashed by an unexpected "windfall". The windfall is from the mining sector in the order of $AU9 billion due to a rapid increase in profits.[24] Upon reading it, I was yet again perturbed and compromised by the reality that I gain from this maddeningly intractable issue. My moral outrage runs into the advantages I indirectly gain from this reality. Attempts by an earlier Federal Government to tax the profits of large mining companies were quickly howled down by industry lobby and interest groups. The mining conglomerates are relentless in advertising how they fulfil their corporate social responsibility to communities, the jobs they create and their importance to the wealth of Australia. They increasingly disparage the influence of the greenies and rush to try to assuage public concerns about the usually hidden costs of a country's and often households' reliance on income from the mining industry. The greenies are environmental activists who are concerned citizens standing up to protect threats against Nature. They are demonised as the threat to industry with some states passing laws banning protesting.[25]

For many citizens, though, the evidence of the threat to the environment is just out of the headlines of the mainstream reporting and advertising. The evidence is off to the side where important media reports and publications paint a disturbing picture for anyone who cares to look. I think Paul Cleary's *Mine-field: The dark side of Australia's resource rush*, places mining environmental impacts on a parallel level of significance to Carson's evidence of insecticide impacts.[26] When I read Cleary's book, I was keeping up with the story that he was talking about in real time. Cleary had met, and subsequently wrote several publications, with Michael Woodley who is a Yindjibarndi man from the northwest of Western Australia. I haven't met Michael in person but we partnered up on a writing project about his peoples' experience.[27] Michael explains how Fortescue Metal Group (FMG) was determined to mine large tracts of their ancestral homelands against the wishes of many of the people. He describes divide and conquer tactics by the company who offered some of the people a relatively small amount of money to support the mining venture. FMG stands to make an inestimable amount of profit from anticipated future mining and gave one group in the split community $AU4 million. This went against the traditional ways the Yindjibarndi People settled disagreements, namely through discussion with each other. The Yindjibarndi People have had to struggle for their land rights for more than a decade, winning some court hearings only to have them appealed by FMG.

Cleary's more recent book *Title fight: How the Yindjibarndi battled and defeated a mining giant*, details this struggle for justice.[28] Its carefully researched chronicle attests to the unequal playing field and unequal economic gains. The unfairness is most stark when a multinational mining company directly negotiates with people who collectively own land that they and their ancestors have lived on for tens of thousands of years. Cleary's account about the Yindjibarndi Peoples' protracted struggle to gain exclusive ownership of their own land unfortunately is not an isolated example. It is unusual, for the success they have achieved is against the odds.

What is happening in Australia is indicative of other resource rich countries around the world. Cleary provides evidence of mining impact on the environment that is on such a scale it is hard to comprehend. It was shocking for me to see the maps of Australia showing the locations of coal, iron ore, gold, uranium, and coal seam gas (CSG) wells in areas of high productivity underground aquifers. The maps show the major pegged sites for these operations, which includes the conventional gas areas and shale gas reserves. One map shows 5,000 of the 40,000 wells projected to be built in Queensland and New South Wales on some of the best farmlands that provide food for the nation.[26] It is not only the number and location of the mines but their increasing size where it is typical for a mine to extract billions of tons of raw materials. Cleary gives the example of Australia's richest woman, Gina Rinehart, whom he calls Australia's iron lady.[26] Rinehart anticipates her mines in the Galilee Basin to produce eight billion tonnes of coal.[26] Cleary describes the mine areas from the air as vast spiderwebs.[26] Such is the enormity of the network of wells, roads, pipelines, and pressurisation stations. He explains that it is even worse beneath the ground where there are unseen equally vast ants' nests like capillaries which all connect to the Ant Queen, in this case, the pressurisation station.[26] It is far worse now a little over ten years on. I think the metaphors of spiderwebs and ant nests are altogether too benign to portray the devastating environmental impacts Cleary is describing. The combined impact of each mining operation makes this a concerning example of violence against Nature. The scale of use of natural resources to access the CSG is hard to grasp. Research shows a direct link between fracking and sinkholes and the polluting of groundwater to the level that it is unusable by local communities.[26] Cleary writes that evidence to a Senate Rural Affairs Committee by CSG companies reported that each fracking event consumes about one million litres of water, as well as sand and enough chemicals to fill two backyard swimming pools.[26] This is truly shocking.

Large scale mining is indicative of the colonial and capitalist economic base to Australian society. Capitalism requires the exploitation of the environment. Poelina, is a First Nation custodian of the Martoowarra (Fitzroy River), which is one of the last wild rivers in Australia. She explains that the capitalist worldview dislocates people from place. In turn, place is dislocated from culture to the extent that people cannot hear, feel or be with Nature. She refers to this dislocation as being emotionally removed and deliberately deaf to Nature's messages.[29] The pull of the dominant economic arguments underpinning such a degradation of land and seascapes can undercut more sustainable income generating industries.[30]

It is seemingly unstoppable. Cleary likens the current mining resource boom in Australia to the gold rush era of early colonial Australia in the 1800s.[26] I think he would agree that we are entering another resource rush in the form of precious metals needed for many initiatives – such as electric cars – that might otherwise contribute to reducing greenhouse gas emissions. Critical minerals such as vanadium, copper, zinc, and cobalt are now highly prized and mining leases have increased in Australia.[31] Mining magnate Andrew Forrest, the CEO of FMG, is vocal about the need for industry to change to this new green approach.[32] There must be money in it and this unfortunately does not bode well for the undue influence of companies such as FMG on governments of the day. Forrest recommended policy pointers to the previous Abbott Federal Government for Aboriginals to do more to help themselves to the benefits of mining.[33] As I mentioned, it is FMG who has been at the centre of one of the most protracted and hard fought legal battles by the Yindjibarndi People in the Pilbara area.

This brings me to an example of an under-appreciated aspect of the unsustainability of environmental degradation, namely the explicitly political nature of the violence. The issue relates to the tendency for mining leases and approvals to be granted by government authorities in areas contested by First Nation owners. The massive Adani coal mine venture in Queensland is a case-in-point. It is expected to produce 40 million tonnes a year in the culturally and ecologically sensitive 8,000 hectare Bimblebox Nature Reserve. The Wangan and Jagalingou Family Council maintain an active struggle against the development. Their views and activism, such as the failed attempt to challenge Adani in the Federal Court, are detailed on their website. They have gained some broader based public support through campaigns such as protests aimed at protecting the black-throated finch habitat which is threatened by the mine development.[34] The Federal Government election of 2019 was purported to have been lost because candidates did not show sufficient regard for the pro-mining communities and interest groups. These groups were arguing for the mine to proceed despite continuing concerns for the financial capacity of Adani and the environmental impacts. Subsequently, the Queensland Government extinguished native title and thereby removed the right of First Nation owners to enter their land for ceremonial purposes and to protest.[35] The Wangan and Jagalingou Family Council resistance continues to this day fearing they will die as a people and a culture if the mine goes ahead.[36, 37] I gained permission to include their struggle in a publication I wrote with Michael Woodley.[38] Going forward, I am keeping a close eye on what is happening with the Adani mine. I remain alert for opportunities to stand with other Australians as allies with all the First Nations in the Galilee Basin to ensure the Adani mine does not get its final approvals. These struggles for eco justice continue even though the evidence is clear that humans' continual use of fossil fuels is overheating the earth.[39]

Governments are not innocent bystanders in the violence of environmental degradation and climate change. It is well-recognised that state and federal levels of government gain from minerals extraction and other uses of the environment for profit by private interests. Taxes and royalties are key sources of income generation. But governments also subsidise industries based on environmental degradation. Gergis claims that Australian governments provided more in-tax breaks for the fossil fuel industries ($AU11.1 billion) than for the Federal Government's Housing Australia Future Fund ($AU10 billion).[39] The picture is more complicated than this with some of the worst environmental disasters occurring with the acquiescence of the government, in spite of warnings from research evidence. One example is the troubling issue of workers at the Wittenoom mine site in Western Australia's northwest contracting asbestosis, an often fatal lung disease. The mining of asbestos – a blue metal – in the Hamersley Ranges in the early 1950s occurred with inadequate protection for the 20,000 workers and locals. Medical officer warnings of health issues for workers were not heeded by the State Government. The slow onset of the terminal disease of asbestosis, meant it was a decades-long unfolding tragedy of immense proportions. Wittenoom was eventually de-gazetted as a town many years after the mining company left, leaving the whole area contaminated and dangerous for people and other animals. Some residents have refused to leave saying it is their home. In 2007, impacted workers from the mine-site led by Bernie Banton won a court case against the James Hardie company for compensation relating to asbestosis related injuries.

In 2022, some fifteen years after the closing of the town, the Western Australian Government passed a bill to give it the legal power to destroy the last of the dwellings and remove the people.[40] More recently, the Banjima First Nation People have won a long struggle for native title over their country. But they have been given a heavily contaminated wasteland with no offers to help remediate it.[40] Worksafe Western Australia argues that the devastation and loss of life are comparable to the Chernobyl and Bhopal catastrophes. They estimate that by

2020 more than 45,000 people, including children, will have died from asbestosis or mesothelioma.[40]

Recounting such a devastating tragedy may seem unnecessarily alarmist. It happened in the last century, but people are still dying from the disease. Governments didn't know better, but in actuality, they did. Well then, surely the government rushed to give affected workers compensation once it was brought to their attention in a way they couldn't ignore by worker activism? No. Surely, we have learnt about such dangers and they aren't happening anymore in Australia? Unfortunately, no. I do not go looking to hear of industry pollution impacting local towns and landscapes, unsafe work conditions, environmental impacts due to development of new mines, and unfair treatment of First Nation People by mining companies. Each time something hits the news, I feel the same broken-heartedness all over again.

This next example has echoes of Hinkley and Erin Brokovich, but it is here in Australia and involves the Federal Government. The Government's direct involvement in environmental harm occurred when The Royal Australian Air Force continued to use toxic retardants in their fire training and safety drills, despite being warned of the dangers for years. The retardant contains perfluoroalkyl polyfluoroalkyl (PFAS) chemicals known to be carcinogenic which leached into nearby streams and waterways of several regional towns across Australia. The impacts are concerning and include whole towns not being able to drink their water.[41] Private citizens have had to take legal action to get some recognition for the harm done.[42]

Then, when it didn't seem possible that more extreme, irretrievable harm could be done by a mining company using loopholes in legislation, the worst did happen. Nation level outrage occurred in 2020 due to the actions of one of Australia's largest mining companies, Rio Tinto. The company destroyed 46,000 year old sacred Indigenous rock shelters in Juukan Gorge in the northwest of Western Australia.[43] A parliamentary inquiry was held requiring Rio Tinto to negotiate compensation with the traditional owners. It is though surely nonsensical to suggest that it is possible to fully repair caves that pre-date the last ice age. This is a loss of world significance. It is troubling to read Pat Dodson, a First Nation Senator, ask how many other similar mining situations are planned which can use legal loopholes to commit further destruction.[43]

Mining companies continue to act with such disdain for nonmaterial and cultural values. I have found being closely involved with one community impacted by mining operations has helped me grasp some of the political, economic, and social complexities involved in matters of environmental injustice. It has helped me not feel so powerless about the overall situation when I have witnessed such sustained community-based resistance and activism. Such resistance and activism has made some inroads into the seemingly intractable influence of mining companies over governments at the cost of people, place, and other animals.

Some situations capture public concern, such as the large-scale death of birds on the southern coast of Western Australia in 2007. A newspaper reported it as the *Day the birds fell dead*.[44] The public outcry led to a swift response by the State Government, but the cause of thousands of birds dying was not found. This was despite the relevant department interviewing local industries and farmers about pesticide and chemical use. It eventually was blamed on toxic wetlands due to algal bloom with the drier winter. Echoes of Carson's warnings still reverberate down the decades. So the Government acted but nothing changed, and no-one took the shared responsibility needed to reduce and remove the use of toxic chemicals from the landscape.

Meanwhile, the long standing and multi-faceted harms caused by Alcoa World Alumina a couple of hundred kilometres south of Perth city were simmering on. No mass public outrage to help save Yarloop. The State Government response continued to be absent or compromised by royalties and lobbying from the mining giant. More than two decades on from the first media reports of pollution by Alcoa and my research, the small town of Yarloop is not recognisable and the whole rural area is profoundly impacted by mining operations. One of the starkest costs is the loss of jarrah forests in a landscape with thin coverage of trees, along the Darling escarpment which runs parallel to the coast, from Perth to the southern coast. Recent media headlines capture the seriousness of the escalation of strip mining for bauxite by Alcoa and Worsley Alumina, with Rio Tinto seeking mining leases in the area – *Mines clear more trees than logging in Western Australia's threatened forests.*[45] Alcoa and Worsley have long term mining leases over 10,000 square kilometres which covers the northern part of the Darling Ranges east and southeast of Perth city. de Kruijff explains that the 250 kilometre area is subject to such an intensive removal of habitat that it threatens the black cockatoos and mainland quokka's survival.[45] Unfortunately, Alcoa World Alumina has its own State Agreement courtesy of the Western Australian Government. The State Agreement protects Alcoa against

Federal Government-level legislation that has been successfully used against developments that threaten endangered and other species.

Whenever I have returned to Western Australia from the east coast and flown in over the Darling Ranges, it has been disturbing to see how little forest remains. When I lived in Bunbury, I joined protests in the 1990s and early 2000s to stop the logging of old growth forests. Western Australia does not log its old forests anymore. This was such a big achievement in a very pro-development state. However, there were other sources of threat to the forests which caused me to join concerned citizens in the coastal areas adjacent to the Darling Ranges. One threat was when urban development was coming at the cost of small corridors of tuart trees – the other hardwood tree unique to Western Australia. At the time, on the coastal plain, a titanium mining company was seeking environmental approval to mine in the Ludlow tuart forest – which was gained at the cost of 1700 tuart trees.[46] I continue to be aghast at how forests are treated as commodities and not as beings with their own right to be. The level of threat and plans to increase strip mining in the Darling Ranges is hard to grasp but it is a major environmental issue in 2023. Western Australia's peak environmental groups – Western Australia Forest Alliance, the Wilderness Society, and the Conservation Council of Western Australia – compiled a significant report called *A Thousand cuts: Mining in the northern jarrah forests* in 2022.[47] It outlines the extremely compromised ecosystem in the northern jarrah forest due to bauxite mining. The situation is aggravated by the cumulative impact from other sources such as urban development, logging, and prescribed burning.[47]

The forest is dying and still the mining rolls on. Does it matter? Do people in the cities know what is happening? Every forest matters on a planetary level through to the individual trees' level where all the nonhuman animals depend on them for their life. When the jarrah forest in Western Australia is gone in this part of the world, they will be lost completely. The botanical name for the jarrah tree is *Eucalyptus marginata*, which can grow to a height of fifty metres with trunk widths of three metres. Their flowers are cone shaped casings that burst open with a scented white flower and the jarrah provides a home for bees, marsupials, and birds. They were logged for their precious red hardwood timber and some are known to be over 500 years old. If you didn't know about the jarrah trees, please watch out for them by lending your support to the peak bodies trying to protect them, even if you live far away.

Needlessly eating our Kin. Feeding the elites' wealth

Entwined with matters of environmental injustice are issues relating to species injustice. There is an illogic about the scale of exploitation and consumption of farmed animals. The killing and eating of other animals, who Haraway calls our Kin, is needless.[48] We don't need to eat other animals' flesh and use their skins, eggs, and other parts of their bodies. In fact, the plant-based alternatives have less impact on climate change caused by global warming.[49] But rational arguments about the cost effectiveness and sustainability of plant-based foods do not sway the public to change their eating habits, even as many take pride in having a meat-free meal once a week.

My moral outrage is not with individual people who eat the flesh of other animals. If I let myself 'go there' I would be constantly angry. Rather, I reserve my moral outrage for extremely wealthy individuals and corporations. Specifically, the elites of Australian society who gain their wealth from the killing of farmed animals. The slaughter of defenceless animals feeds their wealth on a scale which is hard to comprehend. The business elites' profit-driven actions reinforce the continued large-scale exploitation of farmed animals. At the same time, people who are poor cannot afford to eat meat. Few people have the option my family had of sourcing other animals' flesh to survive by going up the bush with a gun and knife as my father did.

I did not know the full story of harm to other animals as a little person growing up in an era when Australia's prosperity was attributed to riding on the sheep's back. It seemed a strange thing to say when I first heard the expression in primary school. The teacher was telling us about the primary industries that made Australia the lucky country. We learnt about how sheeps' wool was highly prized, especially the merino sheep. I knew all about wool because my mother was an amazing knitter. She knitted all our jumpers for us from newborn to teenager. The wool she used was every colour you could imagine. For the longest time before synthetic fibres, my mum would use wool from merino sheep – she bought the best when she could afford it. I was also interested in what my teacher was saying because some of the farming jobs my father and grandfather (on my mother's side) had involved shearing sheep. It was mostly by hand as they were small herds of sheep, and this along with branding shorn sheep, were some of my earliest experiences of

other animals being used by humans. It was stressful to watch
the sheep being sheared. The sheep were treated very firmly,
sometimes roughly, and held against their will on the shearing
shed floor or bench. I've seen shearers become impatient with
sheep as they struggled. Some got cut and were clearly hurt and
uncomfortable. This was very perturbing to witness and no-one
saw anything strange about it or thought to talk with me about
what was happening.

The other vivid memory I have of how intertwined my
family was with using other animals. It happened continuously
throughout my childhood. When we visited my auntie and
uncle, it would be a house overflowing with people as my auntie
had seven children. This meant all us eight kids would have to
top and tail in our cousins' beds and muck in with jobs around
the house. Feeding everyone was a major task. My mum and
auntie were incredible with how they put together meals often
with very little money and only the produce from the vegetable
garden. There was always lots of mashed potatoes and animal
flesh on our plates. We constantly felt hungry after playing
all day. We lined up around an enormous table that couldn't,
despite its size, fit everyone in one sitting. There was no way
the meat would be purchased from the butcher's shop as it was
way too costly. It was, therefore, a key part of our extended
families' survival that my uncle was a rabbiter. This meant he
would set traps down along the nearby river banks. Every day
he would check the traps for captured, and not always dead,
rabbits and other critters unfortunate enough to be caught in
this cruel way. Sometimes a trapped animal had escaped and
the trap was sprung. Other times, another disturbing situation

arose where the trapped animal was nowhere to be seen but had dragged the trap away with them.

So I knew very well where the meat on our dinner plates came from. And just like all the other kids, I ate it all up. We would feed the bones to the dogs at the back door. Nobody ever talked about it being something that was not okay. There was no way in an era of 'children should be seen and not heard', that any protests about not liking cow's liver, sheep's brains, cow's tongues or roast pork, would be entertained. It sat very uncomfortably with me, but I had no language for what the discomfort was. No-one showed me a different way of thinking. Even memories of delightful experiences such as hand feeding baby calves from the nearby dairy when staying at my auntie's were later exposed for hiding a harsh reality. The calves, just a few days old, were removed from their mothers so they would keep producing milk. It was this harsh reality that decades later finally provided me the impetus to become vegan. But this was not until quite recently. I am dismayed to admit this. There were other profound experiences in my childhood that I was slow, and perhaps reluctant, to place squarely in front of me and to recognise the prejudice against other animals who are used for human consumption.

I do not know why I ever thought it was a good idea to go rabbiting with my uncle and older cousins. Why did our parents let that happen? I accepted it as normal and fun to jump on the back of the ute in the early hours as the sun was rising and head out to collect the rabbits. I saw so much suffering that is forever etched in my mind and heart. But I tried to focus on saving the rabbits. Sometimes I was allowed to keep and look after the injured baby rabbits, especially ones my father would bring me from time-to-time back home in George Town. I had a very small hutch on the back lawn for whomever was the current resident rabbit. While many would die from shock, some lived a long time. This became 'my thing', but looking back it was a very powerless gesture to stem the tide of other animal suffering.

I was still in primary school, about seven or eight years of age, when I became increasingly disturbed by the sight of rabbit skins hanging in an old shed down behind my auntie's house. The shed was open on one side and all the walls were full of animals' skins stretched out over U-shaped wire and hanging on nails. When dead rabbits were having their skin removed I was nowhere to be seen but I knew it was happening, along with the butchering of the animals to prepare them for eating. This was a key source of income for my auntie and uncle as they would sell the rabbit skins and animal flesh.

My auntie and uncle also had lots of chickens, as did my mum and dad. Eggs were highly valued and as I got older I realised the chooks were not only kept for their eggs. They are one of the most heavily farmed of all the other animals due to their white flesh. We always had chooks in our backyard. We would have to help clean out their yard, collect the eggs, and would watch as dad would move the whole chook pen set up around the backyard. He would then plant the next lot of vege crops in the just-vacated chook pen. The backyard scale of chicken use was repeated throughout our neighbourhood. It was some time before I came to understand the enormous commercial scale of chicken farming and the horrendous conditions of many of these factories. Even so, as a child, it was perturbing to see my dad killing and plucking chooks and then watching my mum cook them for dinner. I had no idea what happens to most of the male chickens until well into my adult life. How could it take that long when it was obvious there was only ever one rooster in the chook pen?

Nothing was said in school about how baby sheep were killed for their young flesh. Lamb chops were a favourite in my family. While a farmer, my dad would kill and prepare the bodies of sheep and cows much as a butcher would do. He also would go up the bush to hunt kangaroos and rabbits to feed his growing family. This going up the bush was part of my family life even after we moved to George Town and Dad was working at Comalco. It was not questioned and, as I say, it was part of the Australian identity to be a farmer who contributed to the country's wealth. The mining industry was, even then, a key part of the economy but not so lauded or part of the public consciousness and pride.

Meanwhile, the main place we went on family holidays was up the lakes, in the central highlands area of Tasmania. As a big, poor family, fancy holidays in hotels or flying to a city on the mainland were not within reach. It was a big enough deal to pack us all up with the camping gear and travel a couple of hours along very winding steep roads to get to the lakes and set up the camp site. Even on holidays, or rather, especially on holidays, our family life was organised around the killing of other animals. It was, of course, never spoken of in this way. Dad would go fishing along the lake shore line in his own little dingy and, in time, a bigger boat. Some of us kids would go with him. Sometimes we would try to fish on our own little fishing rods. The sight of fish caught by the mouth on a rod was shocking every time but was drowned out by the cheers of others in the family. "Hooray. What a catch." The fish would be placed in buckets of water to flail around in their own distress. Needless to say, we would all line up on logs around the campfire to watch the filleted pieces of fish being fried and then hungrily eat them.

In my childhood naivety, I enjoyed family road trips where we counted the cows and sheep peacefully grazing in ultra green paddocks. They seemed so happy and well cared for. Us kids would struggle to stave off boredom or the discomfort from being packed in the station wagon like sardines. Sometimes we'd count the cows and comment on their different kinds of beautifully coloured coats. There were Friesian, Jersey, and Holstein dairy cows and Bradford and Brahman cows bred for their flesh. If we saw calves and baby lambs there was always great delight. Fast forward, these days I try to avoid driving in the country because I know the picture is not such a happy one. Most of the other animals I see from the car window are being farmed for human consumption. That they don't know it is very cold comfort. I am greatly distressed when travelling behind a truck transporting animals to abattoirs or ports for live animal exports. The last time this happened, a few months ago, it was a truck with layer upon layer of penned chickens. I could hardly breathe when I looked any of them in the face. Their feathers were blowing out of their cages and over my car and other cars behind me. The highway of vehicles rushed on and the hundreds upon hundreds of chickens sped towards their death. They feed a population who perhaps has never met a chicken and held it in their arms. They would be incapable of killing one with their own hands.

There is a rural town not far from the coast which I sometimes have to drive through to visit family way out west. On its outskirts is an enormous white building, very clean, very well maintained . The building has an obscure name of [insert any relevant town's name] Pastoral Company. I didn't realise what it was until, one trip, a large truck carrying cows turned into the property just in front of me. It was an abattoir. The cows were being taken to be slaughtered and they had no choice and no way of escaping. Their innocence and powerlessness have stayed with me. It was just one truck full of other animals of the hundreds and hundreds I have passed on the road over the years, even though I have not lived near an abattoir.

These horror memories coalesce with the trapped rabbits of my childhood, the disappearing chooks from our chook pens, the hand fed calves removed from their mothers, and what I later learned about the baby male calves killed soon after birth. My teachers did not mention what really happened down on the farm. There was no mention of how other animals were denied their right to live their lives without fear and being controlled. In not speaking the full picture of how we treat other animals, us children were ill prepared to question what was happening. It would have made such a difference if a teacher, or another adult, had talked to me about the prejudice that makes killing and eating other animals an okay thing to do. My integrity as a child growing up was so compromised by this silence. I became complicit in the violence against other animals, without my informed consent.

I was fortunate enough to go to university and studied for a Bachelor of Arts. This was despite my working-class background, and despite the social norm that girls work until they get married and have children. My peer group were really nice people whom I met through my boyfriend — they nearly all were studying engineering. So I missed out on the chance to be radicalised by sociology and political science clubs and activism on campus. It was the early 1970s and I was eighteen and very naïve about the social movements sweeping the world, especially the environmental movement and animal rights causes. My first education about the environment occurred because it was (almost) in my backyard when I was at uni in Hobart. I became very aware of and supported the "Save the Franklin River" activist campaign that was raging. It was 1978, and the Tasmanian Government wanted to dam the lower reaches of the river system to generate hydro-electricity. I often went bushwalking in the south west of Tasmania and like many others, realised the preciousness of the World Heritage area and the wild river. Further to the aquatic animals of the river, other animals such as platypus, wallabies, quolls, and yellow-tailed cockatoos relied on the river for their survival. I understood the significance of this one river remaining wild in its own right. But I did not realise so many rivers were under threat globally. The threats were due to the environmental degradation that was happening at the time and which has continued to accelerate since then.

While at uni, I did not know a single person who was vegetarian and didn't know the word veganism and how it was different to vegetarianism. Nevertheless, I stopped eating the flesh of cows, sheep, kangaroos, rabbits, and chickens. But, for another few years, I still ate sea animals. Much later on I stopped eating eggs, honey and dairy products. It was interesting to me how offended people became if I declined to eat animal flesh at parties or when out having a meal with them. This was a pattern that continued for the rest of my life. Being vegetarian was a small price to pay for easing my conscience a little as soon as I had some autonomy to make such decisions. I went on to do a social work degree and this was the best decision I ever made. It has shaped who I am in so many ways. But, as I mentioned before, there was almost no room in any conversation or lecture for other animals and injustices done to them. I remained passive and unaware of the scale of violence to farm animals in particular. I comforted myself thinking that being vegetarian was my contribution to lessening harm to other animals.

As a young adult, though, I did not miss the womens' movement, and found it was a compatible fit with my degree in social work. I could write about gender inequality in assignments and discuss it with other students. I've been a feminist ever since and re-read my early childhood experiences through the lens of sexism, thanks to Germaine Greer, and classism, thanks to Karl Marx. Feminist writers changed my sense of who I was as a woman. No wonder I felt such frustration with the social norms I had struggled with – that a 'woman's place is in the home' and that 'women are the weaker sex'. Greer's provocative ideas blew my mind and made me question everything. She wrote that women needed to embrace their sexuality and agency in the world.[50] Women should feel free to be fully alive and able to know and love the earth.[50] She understood that many women were far from free, and in fact were often subjected to violence and silenced by prejudicial social norms.[50]

While I studied Marx in a sociology class, his writing was pretty hard to grasp. Nevertheless, I found his idea that the economic base of a society largely shapes social relations really inspiring.[51] In 1859, he wrote that these economic forces not only shape social relations but shape the peoples' consciousness.[51]

These ideas resonated partly because they aligned with how my father's work strongly influenced my childhood. In turn, being poor collapsed many life choices for my parents and some of us children, especially the girls. Our working class circumstances were influential in my family, as we saw ourselves as unworthy and second-class citizens. I have continued to hold a feminist-Marxist view of inequality in society ever since. As you can see, it is no accident that I became a social worker.

I lived in an intentional community for several years in my twenties. I found for the first time other people who were vegetarians and feminists or pro-feminism. Our collectively-owned place was an old dairy farm where we cultivated small crops for the Brisbane markets and local outlets in the Kin Kin area on the Sunshine Coast. It was with these like-minded people that I found my voice, and felt that I belonged somewhere with others who lived in a socially conscious and nonviolent way. We didn't have domestic animals or pets as a commitment to create a safe place for wild animals. Many nights, I would awake in my cabin, which was on a hillside set away from the main farm house, and find large male kangaroos fighting on my verandah. My cabin's double glass doors were always open and it was quite an intense experience to say the least. Sometimes kangaroos came into my cabin but not usually when they were fighting. It was my closest connection to other animals in my life other than fleeting contacts and sightings when bushwalking in Tasmania or when travelling by road.

Experiencing wildlife while travelling is a very stressful scenario, though. More often than not, the encounters were with dead animals who were hit by cars and trucks. There were some places where the roadkills were so prevalent that it was unbearable to witness. I do everything I can to avoid roads where I know many wild animals die. This does nothing to help them, though. Some animals and birds take advantage of the roadkills. One of the most amazing sights is of wedge-tailed eagles feasting on another animal's carcass on the road side. I saw these enormous birds of prey up close when I have slowed my car down to avoid hurting them. So impressive. They would be more than capable of surviving without humans causing the deaths of other animals.

I was teaching in social work many years later when I discovered Mies and Shiva's important book *Eco-feminism*.[52] This had quite an impact on how I understood who mattered in the world. They explained how the human bias against other animals parallels sexism towards nondominant gender and sexual identity groups. I had not yet grasped the scale of discrimination against other species. I knew that, globally, violence against women was recognised as a major cause of ill health and premature death. Women's liberation has not yet enabled the liberation of millions of women and their children. Mies and Shiva's ideas deeply shaped my thinking of the pervasiveness of violence caused by inequalities that cross species boundaries, whomever is targeted. The ideas of Nature as a commodity, of other animals as livestock for humans' use and of women as men's chattels, are all part of the same patriarchal, colonialist and capitalist system of oppression. This system literally trades in heartbreak.

In 1997, I was captivated by the international headlines of McDonald's court case for cruelty to other animals it used in producing burgers and other products. It was the first time I saw it was possible to hold a large multi-national company accountable for where it sourced its animals. It was the longest running trial in Britain at the time and the 'McLibel' trial captured headlines in the print media for years. Two private individuals, a part-time bartender and an unemployed postman, were taken to court by McDonalds for claims they made in a pamphlet they distributed. McDonalds was awarded damages but were found to be responsible for cruelty to animals in their supply chain and for exploiting children by underpaying young people in their stores. What was so significant was how the judge understood what needed to be considered in making their decision. Lyall reported the verdict in *The New York Times* and recounted how the decision recognised the interconnectedness between slave labour wages for its workers, the farming of cows for McDonald's burger, the loss of farmlands for other uses, and the loss of forests and the natural environment.[53] It planted a seed of hope in me that changing systems of oppression against other animals and the environment was possible. But the legal decision has not stopped the McDonaldisation of the world ever since. Ritzer describes the idea of McDonaldisation as how the efficiency and control of McDonald's production line processes in their fast food chains have been adopted throughout Western societies.[54]

Our moral integrity as a society is compromised in many ways with regard to farmed animals. The mass slaughter of other animals is the main stain on our collective character and capacity to love all beings. Not only are other animals treated as objects for humans' use, but, in doing so, humans suffer as well. But only some groups of humans suffer and not usually by paying the price of their lives. As just one example, typically, people who are migrants or unskilled workers from poor local towns are employed in abattoirs. The workers experience trauma from the violence they enact on other distressed animals.[55] Some workers become desensitised. Eaglehawk makes the link between racism, the exploitation of other animals, and toxic masculinity which occurs in patriarchal societies.[49] Toxic masculinity refers to an idealised image or stereotype of the Australian male as macho, violent, and strong. As with all idealised images, it is not representative of all males. The relevance here is that the predominantly male occupation of slaughtering other animals in abattoirs mirrors the violence being committed by men against women.[49] This echoes back to my own childhood experience of domestic violence by my father and the consumption of other animals who were captured and killed by him and other male relatives. My grandfather farmed animals for their milk and hunted wild animals for their flesh. He also committed domestic violence towards his family, as well as other forms of violence against some of his children. I'm not saying this is a causal link, that it explains everything, but it is disturbing that it holds true in many instances. Further, there are more layers to who is harmed in households where male toxicity and dominance of other people is occurring in the form of domestic violence. It is not usually recognised that pets and domestic animals can be targets of violence as well. Sometimes they are used as pawns to gain compliance of family members, or left when human victims flee the household.[56]

Some people are greatly advantaged by the use of other animals. Globally, large-scale farming involves the main group of animals who endure extreme control over their lives, separation from their young and, sometimes, others in their social group. They are routinely slaughtered when it is optimal for the farmer's bottom-line of costs and profits. The scale of loss of farm animals is so enormous it is almost meaningless to place a number on the loss. Even when the animals are alive, the level of care provided to them can be minimal or nonexistent, especially in industrialised facilities. Coulter gives the example of a sick pig in a barn of 1,000 pigs who is unlikely to receive medical care.[57] Rather, they may be left to die, be killed, or sent to an abattoir. Many animals arrive at abattoirs injured, unhealthy, and distressed.[57] I want to momentarily bring a focus to one pig, one life, one sentient being who suffered and died, and how no one human acted to show care and compassion. In that one pig's close proximity were other pigs who would have been distressed with the pig's suffering but no one acted to show care and compassion. Maybe if we could feel something of what this one pig went through, just maybe more humans would change away from eating other animals.

When not deprived of movement and association with their Kin, farm animals provide care, comfort, and companionship to each other. Almost without exception, farm animal mothers are denied the opportunity to care for their babies. Mother cows bred for their flesh are allowed to keep their young for a longer period until they are due to be slaughtered. All farm animals are slaughtered before the natural end of their lives. Farmed chickens have a life expectancy of no more than three months, while their natural life expectancy can be as long as ten or more years. Research has been slow to show that other animals are caring, intelligent, and active in their life-seeking behaviours. Yet it is unlikely that any amount of research will pierce through the mass human moral amnesia that allows the killing to continue.

A generational change happened in my family thanks to my own daughter. She grew up in a household with no violence or coercion, where she was treated as an equal person, and involved in all decisions which affected her. My daughter was vegetarian from the earliest of times even though there was no pressure on her to be so. In her early twenties, when she was at university, she made the decision to become vegan after hearing some very impactful arguments from a peer in one of her classes. This precipitated a discussion with me when she got home as to why I wasn't vegan. I had no good reason and changed instantly. I remain mortified that it took me so long, and that it took my own child to show me my own ethics were not up to scratch despite all my preaching as a social work lecturer. I instantly felt more congruent with my feelings and beliefs. The pain in my heart eased off a little. More than I thought possible. Nevertheless, I knew it wasn't the answer to other animal suffering as it was occurring on such an enormous scale and was so entrenched in most societies on the planet. But I didn't know what else to do. That was about eight years ago, and now I understand how the animal industrial complex that Kristy Alger writes about. It requires much more of practising vegans than not eating animals, or using them in any way against their will or interests.[58]

I met Kristy when she approached my daughter to have her book on other animals published by *Revolutionaries*. Kristy's book was absolutely mind-blowing for me. It all made so much sense. She was writing about her experiences of trying to advocate for farmed animals. Sometimes Kristy was rescuing them literally from death's door in Tasmania, my home state, which made her work all the more impactful. She placed my childhood experiences of harm to other animals squarely in a sophisticated political analysis of a too-cosy relationship between the government and industries based on the use and killing of farmed animals. I readily recognised her writing and the activism she was drawing upon as an act of enormous courage as she called out some of the biggest businesses in the farming sector.

Alger develops her argument by identifying the role played by what she calls the carceral state.[58] The carceral state refers to the many ways power is used to control undesirable humans' behaviour to create, what Foucault calls, docile bodies. This idea helps explain the collective moral amnesia of humans who eat and, in other ways, use and gain from other animals. This moral amnesia is reinforced by dominant ideas of the elites, for example, '(animal) meat is good for your health', 'animals are killed humanely', 'animals aren't like us, they don't feel pain', and so on. Alger draws a potent parallel with Foucault's idea of the prison as an example of total control of prisoners and modern intensive farming systems.[58] The carceral state is the interconnected, mutually reinforcing, self-serving interests of the elites of industry, government, and social institutions. Intensive, large-scale farming is just one type of mechanism of control undertaken for wealth creation, often to extreme levels of profit or political advantage. Alger details this dominant power structure and how it operates, all the while showing how, at every turn, the farmed animals are of central interest as a commodity even as they are hidden from the public.[58] Sometimes other animals are hidden in plain sight – sometimes in open paddocks or free ranging across vast areas of unfenced bushland. Mostly, though, they are hidden from public sensibilities – transported in closed panel trucks and processed in abattoirs in the country somewhere. Alger goes on to suggest that farm animals are treated like criminals because of their animality.[58] This is profoundly troubling as it places animals in an unwinnable, highly exploitative relationship with humans. She explains that there is nothing animals can do to avoid being at risk of violence because they are animals in a world dominated by humans.[58]

Large-scale farming of other animals is on par with the mining sector in terms of its significance to the Australian economy. Gina Rinehart, Australia's richest person, makes her estimated $US35.9 billion wealth from mining and large-scale animal farming. She owns more than 20 beef and agricultural properties that comprise 1.5% of Australia's land mass. One property is bigger than Denmark. In 2016, Rinehart claimed to have a cattle herd of over 300,000 animals across these properties.[59] She has continued since that time to build her industrial-sized empire where some of her wealth is based on the lives of other animals. But what is shown in the media are the prizes she wins for the quality of the wagyu beef she breeds.[60] A quick Google search shows how Rinehart spends her money on palatial properties and a $AU20 million penthouse on the luxury cruise liner, The World. Extreme wealth by the few holds the mass scale slaughter of other animals in place, as it becomes integral to the economic wealth of the country. The powerlessness of farmed animals cannot be more stark.

In 2017, Rinehart was reported to have signed a deal with a Chinese company to ship in the order of 300,000 live cattle to China each year.[61] The number of animals was expected to rise to 800,000 by 2020. That such a wealthy person and her company could regard this deal with the Chinese company as an appropriate transaction is very concerning. At the time, another cattle company owned by FMG mining magnate Andrew Forrest, declined to be involved in Rinehart's business deal. A journalist for *The Australian* reported that Forrest, who owns several cattle stations, believed it was better to process the animals in Australia than treat the country as a cattle yard for other countries.[61]

Rinehart's ethics are instrumentalist and focused on business profitability. Forrest's are focused in the same way, but cloaked in it being an ethical good for local employment to slaughter and process the flesh of farm animals in Australia. Neither mention publicly the suffering of animals in the live export industry or as a result of their farming practices in Australia. This is where my moral outrage gets focussed, on the wealthy who make even more wealth by the exploitation of farm animals, in tandem with exploitation of the environment in their mining leases.

Even so, these two business elites' combined impact is a small part of a very large sector of the farming industrial complex in Australia. Live animal exports are very troubling for the known harm to animals during transportation. Globally, each year, it is estimated that two billion animals are subjected to being traded in the live export marketplace. This equates with five million animals being transported every day.[62] In Australia, the live animal transport industry almost collapsed in 2017 when the current affairs program, *60 Minutes*, ran an exposé of the cruelty inflicted on sheep being exported to the Middle East.[63] The trade was ceased for a period of time while an investigation was undertaken amid a public outcry over the images of extreme cruelty. Since that time, the Western Australian Government has improved its welfare standards but continues to support the industry. Nevertheless, in a significant development, the Federal Government decided to phase out the entire live sheep export trade.[64] This is a significant decision and is likely to be strongly resisted by industry groups.

My own moral amnesia and slowness to act to avoid harming other animals is a case-in-point. It remains one of the biggest regrets of my life that I have only in recent years become vegan. Alger reminds vegans that not causing harm to other animals is only one aspect of what is required. Change won't happen until the entire animal industrial complex is dismantled. My journey to becoming vegan and Alger's influence on my thinking combine to keep me from being complacent, and also from being judgemental towards other people who eat and use other animals.

The problem with eco injustice

Violence and lovelessness occur in relationships and are felt in bodies and hearts. Human bodies and hearts. Other animals' bodies and hearts. Nature's bodies and hearts. Wherever lovelessness caused by violence is present or threatened, injustice is occurring. The problem with eco injustice is how the various types of violence for different social and species minority status groups can become entangled and more difficult to challenge. When the entanglement is compounded by degradation of the natural environment, it becomes extremely difficult to imagine a different way of being with other animals and Nature. If there was no injustice between humans, there would be a greater capacity by humans as a species to address the injustice for some species groups such as farmed animals. Some writers have argued the other way around. That is, there is an argument that the unfair treatment of some other animals is the root violence and injustice. This means that until humans stop slaughtering vast numbers of defenceless animals every day, there will be no peace and justice in the world.

The lovelessness for other animals, especially farmed animals, is evidence of the denial of their right to be free of exploitation, their right to safety and care. The denial of farmed animals' equal moral worth underpins the denial of their rights. Humans do not eat animals they love. In denying other animals the right to be loved, we as humans are detracting from our own moral capacity. The baseline multispecies moral capacity is to show mercy for more vulnerable beings.

The evidence of lovelessness and violence against Nature is building and covers all aspects of the adverse impacts on the natural world. Humans as the dominant species hold a collective responsibility for the injustices so caused. These injustices against Nature have begun to change the ability of Nature to re-balance and to sustain life. At the same time, some groups of humans, including governments, and some owners of private companies, hold higher orders of responsibility for the injustices being committed. Extreme wealth derived from the exploitation of Nature and other animals needs to be challenged as morally unsound. This is because, as the base for an economic system, extreme wealth corrupts all citizens, even those who are poor and disenfranchised. Capitalism requires the inequality of minority status groups and species. The problem with wealth derived from use of other animals and exploitation of Nature is that it is a form of violence that breeds and needs injustice.

Gergis explains that the ecological crisis is now so serious and all-pervasive that it is increasingly difficult to know what to say as the mounting evidence is alarming.[39] She writes that a failure of leadership exists among our leaders in government, as they collude with industry's profit driven imperatives. This is occurring despite the mountain of evidence that products from industry are destroying the planet.[39] The fossil fuel industries are her focus for good reason, with Australia planning to develop its gas resources in the next decades to become the biggest producer globally. Gergis is aware that it will be hard for Australia to close down existing, and not start up, nonrenewable energy sources.[39] It will also be hard for the animal industrial complex to be closed down. The vested interests are so entwined and mutually reinforcing, and the public insufficiently galvanised to pressure the government. The challenges in moving to sustainable energy and nonexploitative food sources are not comparable with how hard it will be when the entire life-support system of the planet collapses. The costs will be felt far and wide, and by all species and natural entities, but more so for the most vulnerable people, other animals and ecosystems.

Broken-heartedness

WANT TO UNDERSTAND what can be done to mend our own hearts and those of other broken-hearted people. What can be done in the face of injustice and violence done to us and others? What can we do for ourselves? How can we support someone who has a broken heart? And what of other animals' broken hearts, or Nature's broken-heartedness? I have come to understand the importance of broken-heartedness as a way to describe the impact of complex, interconnected experiences of violence. I want to create a theory of love, a theory that guides us in addressing lovelessness caused by violence and injustice. When I think about what living without love feels and looks like, it can take many forms and can involve big, devastating feelings. It can be exhausting, even life threatening, to have intense feelings of lovelessness. Denial of such feelings can be a way of coping with how painful they can sometimes be. Living without love impacts our bodies, places, and relationships with others.

The problem is lovelessness.
The result is broken-heartedness.
The answer is love.

Broken-heartedness refers to deep distress caused by experiences based on a lack of love. The lack of love due to violence and injustice is perhaps the deepest of all the types of heart wounding. It is a moral distress at being treated unfairly and in harmful ways. It is the deep agony of not being treated as someone deserving of love. This moral distress is intricately expressed in adverse ways in a person's body, health, relationships, dreams, and ability to flourish in the world. A theory of love needs to be expansive; to be inclusive of the diversity of broken-hearted experiences. It also needs to be focused enough to give us a sense of hope. Hope that there is something we can do to ease or address the pain and loss.

As a child, I had an abiding experience of not having a voice, of not being seen and heard. When this invisibility was coupled with being misjudged, it had deep ramifications for me while I was growing up. I would now use the word, broken-hearted, as a more encompassing way of describing the impact a lack of voice has on a person, and how their situation came to be in the first place. The silence that comes with not being seen, heard, and validated is often part of the experience of being broken-hearted. In the silence, it becomes an experience with no name. It is not spoken, not acknowledged, and thereby not addressed. My personal experiences gained a political language when I read Freire's *Pedagogy of the oppressed*.[1] Freire argues that members of oppressed (minority status) groups are subject to a culture of silence about the injustices they are experiencing.[1] The injustice is kept in place by dominant groups' vested interests in maintaining inequality. He developed an internationally recognised approach to education based on a partnership with poor and illiterate people in Brazil. Freire treated the people as active knowing subjects, not empty vessels to be filled with information by experts. Together Freire, the farmers, and villagers built a shared language to understand their world.[1] He worked with them to enable them to read and write. This helped to break the silence and name the unfair treatment they experienced from landowners. In this way, Freire's grassroots method of education gave people access to political rights and power. This is because the right to vote was linked to the ability to read and write.

For part of my Masters degree, I explored the relevance of Freire's idea of *conscientisation* for social work practice. It approximately translates as critical consciousness linked with critical action to change the world.[1] I facilitated some research using a group-based co-operative inquiry with women who felt disempowered. Their culture of silence existed by virtue of gender inequality. My own coming to voice – as both a social worker and as a woman – was also enabled by sharing and learning with the women in the space afforded by the research. It was this research that has inspired me ever since to form groups around shared concerns for both personal and group empowerment. Growing up in a big family had an unexpected gift of feeling at home in groups of people grappling with tough times. Sometimes in my work this toughness was about peoples' relationships with each other as family members or work teams. These are dynamics I am quite familiar with.

Some years later, I vividly recall the moment when the idea of broken-heartedness took on special meaning for me in my professional life. A doctoral student, whom I shall call Sandra, embarked on her research while we were both colleagues in the public mental health service. She had approached me for some early guidance on her research topic. In time, I became one of her research supervisors once we were both academics. Before Sandra started an academic career in nursing, she was a highly experienced mental health clinician. Part of her role was training mental health nurses in the technical and safety procedures for applying ECT to mental health patients. It was seen as best practice, and the efficacy of the treatment was not substantially questioned. Fast forward to the focus of Sandra's research on understanding how women come to make the decision to have ECT. This involved interviewing a number of women about their experiences. A pivotal moment for Sandra was her realisation that the memory loss related to the sense of identity and harm they were describing was irrefutable. As such, the research called into question Sandra's professional integrity in her previous role. Sandra came to the decision that she would never again promote ECT. Her research detailed issues arising from ECT for the women that had not been previously understood, including enduring memory and identity losses.[2]

When Sandra was trying to find a language to describe the womens' experiences, she struggled to find a nonmedical and nondeficit descriptor. After close readings of their stories, we came to the realisation that they were, in essence, broken-hearted. No one had previously asked them how they were faring after having ECT. When they were eventually asked, they each said they had felt silenced and invalidated. This was when a piece of the puzzle fell into place for me. Broken-heartedness seemed an excellent fit even though it was not discussed in the research literature or directly by the research participants.

As part of her doctoral candidature, Sandra presented her research findings to her peers at the university. A respected senior nurse academic in the audience responded by agreeing quickly when Sandra used the term broken-hearted. The academic explained that medical research showed that broken-heartedness had direct links to trauma experiences. That caused an *AHA!* moment for me. Of course. The women had been hurt in a number of ways. For example, when they were told by the treating team there was no other option for them or when they were told there are no side effects to ECT. They had sought help in states of desperation and had become worse off for doing so. The women were left to their own devices with no follow-up on discharge from hospital. There were side-effects, including one of a harmful loss of memory related to their identities as women. Sandra heard them when no-one else had.

Broken-heartedness is a word that has been in my mind since that time, but not as foremost as it is now in this book. I have come to use it as I am trying to find a way of explaining why love really matters. Love matters in all places and relationships but especially where violence and trauma have occurred. Upon reflection – during my childhood and my career as a social worker – it is a word that has so much meaning and captures my own and others' lived experiences. Only now, as I write, am I understanding how my childhood can be described as one of broken-heartedness. I also recognise the relevance of the concept for describing the experiences of so many of the people I have engaged with as a social worker. They would often, in fact, say they had a broken heart. It seemed to be a word that people identified with and felt able to use to tell their stories. Even so, I did not make the links across the stories I was hearing. As a result, I possibly missed opportunities to understand the depth and embodied impact of trying to live with a broken heart.

My understanding of broken-heartedness has some similarities to its popular usage. Dictionaries typically describe broken-heartedness as deep sorrowful feelings caused by the loss of a loved one, usually by death, and include synonyms such as heartache and grief.[3] On social media, one of the most familiar emojis is the image of a stylised heart with a jagged break through its middle. I went in search of how the idea of broken-heartedness was depicted in popular books. It soon became evident that there is an enormous amount written about broken hearts. A number of websites promote a selection of books for getting over a broken heart. For example, Goodreads packages its *Broken hearts book list* in themes such as love, and those who can pierce the heart; broken hearts; healing from divorce; and epic romances.[4]

Perhaps what was more surprising to me was that some print media sources also promote a range of books for the public. In 2022, *The New York Times* ran a headline stating, *Books for broken hearts. Feeling like you've kissed too many frogs? Given up on love altogether? These books might provide some escape this Valentine's Day.*[5] But, then again, such promotions are not surprising given the commercialisation of love in western societies, especially romantic love.[6] Many offerings were preoccupied with familial or intimate loss in interpersonal relationships.[7] The focus is on how to mend your own broken heart with practical tips and guidelines, to transform from "breakdown" to "breakthrough".[8] There is also, sometimes, the promise of how to find the perfect lover after heartbreak.[9] The book reviews show how many people enjoy the read, and how much they gain from these types of publications. Often referred to as pop psychology, it is perhaps too easy to critique this genre of writing for public consumption. Certainly there is a need for the reader to be discerning in deciding what to read. But I do think it is important that we seek to make complex experiences accessible to the public. When these offerings are located in accounts of lived experiences, they can become vital in enabling readers to see themselves in others, and to find a sense of validation with their own experience.

In this book, I am more interested in approaching the idea of broken-heartedness in less of a psychology-only focussed way, and more of a sociological and ecological way. It is perhaps more accurate to say that I aim to include the psychological and emotional dimensions of broken-heartedness through the lens of an understanding of the individual in society. C. W. Mills argues that we need to cultivate a sociological imagination.[10] He explains that it is not enough to focus on the private troubles of an individual. Rather, we can understand their experience as a public issue and, therefore, about society.[10] This is where persisting patterns of loss and harm are identified and need to be addressed. When hearts are broken because of a loved one's death – whether it be from an illness such as cancer or otherwise – it is a deeply personal experience. I have known this loss. When thousands of people die from cancer, it becomes a matter of public concern. There is a need to understand the causes of the different types of cancer and, furthermore, to educate the public on how to avoid any risk factors.[11] When the cancer is asbestosis caused by unsafe mining practices, it is a tragedy for the workers and their loved ones. It is also a concerning public issue that requires accountability and redress by industry and government. As Bernie Banton showed in relation to James Hardies' liability for asbestosis related deaths, too often it is the workers themselves who are left to seek justice.[12] Asbestosis is definitely a public issue and a matter of injustice.

The concept of the ecological imagination extends on the sociological imagination. It weaves together matters relating to other animals and Nature to enfold humans into the tapestry of life on the planet.[13] Humans' wellbeing and very survival is interdependent with Nature's wellbeing and survival.[14] It might seem strange to think of Nature as being broken-hearted. But a heavily polluted river due to toxic runoff from factories, mining, and farm pesticides, will struggle to survive. The water cannot be used by humans, the fish die, and the old gum trees are threatened in their thousands. In one situation, a million native fish died due to a combination of over extracting of water for irrigation and drought.[15] In another, as I write, millions of fish are dying from unknown causes in the Minnidere River in New South Wales.[16] In both devastating situations, the loss of life and vital ingredients for life provided by Nature parallel human experiences of broken-heartedness. In the examples of asbestosis and polluted rivers, there is an injustice done, often despite the available research and knowledge. There is international research on the dangers of asbestos, and climate change research on environmental impacts of severe weather events.[17,18] Carolyn Noble explains that many disadvantaged groups are disproportionately harmed by capitalism and the related inequality that comes from economic activity.[19] Everyone in Nature is impacted, including humans and other animals. This intersection of factors due to human activity can cause broken-heartedness for the sentient beings and natural entities impacted, and for people who witness and care about the harms caused.

I like Dorothy Smith's approach to sociology, where she places peoples' stories and experiences at the centre of any exploration of society.[20] Smith argues that we need to consider the material nature of reality which includes the fact that we live in physical bodies that are located in time, place, and history. I agree with Smith that there is one main task of standpoint sociological research and theorising in a patriarchal society. It is to stand my ground and avoid being subdued by the dominant discourses of ruling elites when theorising about peoples' lived experiences.[20]

I think the term broken-heartedness is useful because it brings the focus onto how the harms and losses have created an impact on the diversity of peoples' lived experiences. What it means for each person cannot be known by others, but needs to be related by the person with the broken-heart. Their story is theirs to tell and interpret. I personally do not take too well to others presuming to know me and what my experiences mean. It is why I like this idea of broken-heartedness, as it places our experiences in our bodies and our own meaning-making. Through telling our story we might, if listened to with love and kindness, find ways to heal our own hearts. The word broken-heartedness invites an empathic response because everyone has had a broken heart and can thereby relate in some way to another's experience.

Thus, I am thinking that broken-heartedness anchors experiences of loss and harm in our human bodies. It is also experienced in other animals' bodies, as well as Nature's bodies and entities. Embodiment, or materiality and physicality, is often referred to as the biological nature of sentient beings and other entities. Noble explains that our human bodies are co-constituted through interactions with a myriad of bodily natures, such as the water we drink, the food we eat, and the micro-organisms we share.[19] This is important in recognising humans are not the only beings with agency in creating the world. Humans are not alone in feeling broken-hearted or showing signs of loss of vitality and bodily integrity when harmed. I lived for much of my adult life without deeply understanding that Nature has agency – such was the limitation of being overly human focused. An intriguing example of the life force and similarity between humans and other sentient beings is provided by the work of forest ecologist Suzanne Simard. Her research shows that trees communicate with each other, and do so in a way very similar to human brains.[21] The trees communicate by using chemical signals – similar to human neurotransmitters – which travel across fungal membranes.[21] Simard's work shifted my view of plant based life, and made me confront my own ignorance about their agency, including the intelligence of, in this instance, trees.

Broken-heartedness for humans can present as heart failures or what are typically called heart attacks. Chronic heart disease is among the highest causes of death in Australia and other westernised countries. What's going on when people have heart attacks at the physical level is complex and not the same for everybody. Research shows that there is a direct link between trauma and severe physiological effects in the body, including the heart.[22] In medical terms, it is referred to as takotsubo, stress-induced cardiomyopathy – otherwise known as broken heart syndrome – where a sudden shock weakens the heart muscle.[23] Shayne cites research which shows that it is mainly experienced by women between the ages of 58 and 75.[24] There is a link between interpersonal violence against women and serious heart disease which has only been exacerbated by the socio-economic stressors of the COVID-19 pandemic.[25] This would suggest a much broader demographic of people impacted by broken heart syndrome not captured by medically focused research. Statistics on domestic violence are devastating, showing it to be a major health issue for women and girls internationally. More than 23% of women in Australia are subjected to what one writer has called "domestic terrorism".[26, 27] Domestic violence can be experienced as broken-heartedness.

Braden explains that the broken heart experience reflects the relationship between the brain and the body in what is termed heart-brain coherence.[28] He writes that the electrical signals from the heart influence the brain's chemical responses throughout the body.[28] Deep loss or threat to life can cause an increase of cortisol and adrenaline in the body, which triggers the survival fight-or-flight response. If this is an ongoing situation of trauma, the impact on a person's body can be extreme and, in itself, life-threatening, or at least increase the risk of health issues.[28] Research has also established what many of us already know from our own experiences. Namely, that depression and other mental health challenges can impact the body and cause what are called co-morbid conditions – for example, depression and coronary heart disease.[29] In terms of health risk factors, depression can have similar impacts on the heart as smoking, high cholesterol levels, and high blood pressure.[30]

When someone says "a person has died of a broken heart", I believe that's exactly what has happened. When the physical heart is broken, this often aligns with an emotionally broken heart. There are deep, sad, abiding feelings of distress, which I think can intensify experiences of harm for the person that are very hard to survive. Given that there is medical evidence of the link between physical harm to the heart and stressful life circumstances, it is important to not shy away from addressing the sources of harm and violence. In 2015, a Queensland farmer, George Bender, died by suicide after a long struggle to protect his farm in Chinchilla from a coal seam gas company. The company was poised to start building wells on his land against his wishes. His family told the media that he died of a broken heart.[31] This is a situation where the extreme pressure placed on the farmer by the gas company was of an order that it was coercive, and caused deep pain in the form of loss of hope and the will to live. A person's physical-emotional heart is a sensitive barometer of their social circumstances. The circumstances need their own attention to address broken-heartedness. The meaning a person makes of their situation of being unfairly treated is experienced as emotions, which become embedded in their bodies and influence how they respond.

My treatise on the need for revolutionary love can be understood, in part, by considering how a lack of love can be heart-breaking. I have suggested this is especially so if that lack of love is related to an experience of injustice or trauma caused by someone hurting another. This is a specific way of thinking about broken-heartedness that can cause very deep wounds in our hearts, and can impact our ability to survive and flourish in the world. This is because love cannot flourish in unsafe situations. Love is a necessary ingredient for life. It is part of the planetary life force.[32] The hardest thing is to believe in love in its absence. The hardest of experiences is when there is injustice and violence done to people. Understanding why broken-heartedness occurs is the first step in discerning what is needed, and who needs to act, to address the harm and loss. Broken-heartedness has many facets to it. People can die of broken-heartedness. But also, people can live for a very long time – or periods of time at least – with a broken heart. It may not even be recognised by others or be called that by the person. Yet it is incredible to me that people can live with a broken heart, and can still be making an amazing contribution in the world. I will never forget reading the remarkable story of Izzeldin Abuelaish from Gaza. Izzeldin continued practising as a doctor, treating both Palestinians and Israelis, after his home was bombed and his daughters and a relative were killed by the Israelis in 2009. His book *I shall not hate* is a detailed account of his life and career, and the heartbreak that he nursed as he worked for peace and understanding.[33]

In telling you some of my experiences with domestic violence as a child, I have demonstrated how lovelessness is caused by violence. Much of my professional story has involved working in mental health systems where violence occurred in the name of care. The most extreme form of organisational violence is expressed in the seclusion and restraint of mental patients. There is a lack of love when systems of care condone restrictive practices which are known to add to patients' trauma. In turn, many mental health practitioners experience bullying and scapegoating in a system which is not organised to be trauma-informed and safe. The exploitation and mass scale destruction of landscapes by mining for natural resources is an example of violence done to Nature. Whole ecosystems collapse, whole species of animals and birds disappear, and contamination stains the landscapes when the mining companies leave. The lack of love for Nature has produced many paths to global warming and all its related violences and unsustainability. Humans' experience of eco-anxiety is related to Nature's broken-heartedness. Adams explains that eco-anxiety is due to extreme worry about climate change and concern for what is happening to the planet.[34] It is a reasonable response to such a cataclysmic situation. The farming industrial complex makes a profit from the killing of millions of farmed animals a day across the planet. The scale is so vast as to be unfathomable. Human bias against some animals causes lovelessness, which enables violence against them to be committed without any guilt and little condemnation from society.

The troubling gift of broken-heartedness

Lovelessness is experienced as broken-heartedness. Violence causes broken-heartedness. Injustices of all kinds cause broken-heartedness. The gift of feeling broken-hearted is that something has really mattered. This is not an argument that broken-heartedness, therefore, is okay. Somehow, that broken-heartedness is inevitable, that this is how life is. But it is quite the opposite. It is a troubling gift – a gift born of unwelcome pain, loss, and trauma.

Nevertheless, it is the case that when something really matters, there is hope in that. There is hope that someone will do something to make it better. Broken hearts can be mended. Broken hearts that are not mattering to anyone become more broken. Extreme acts of violence and injustice occur from lovelessness. People die, or live a half-life, due to lovelessness.

Humans as a species are surely doomed when we do not care if someone is broken-hearted. Being willing to recognise broken-heartedness in others is the first step towards love and away from lovelessness. People can be broken-hearted witnessing others' heartache. If we are broken-hearted ourselves, the willingness to pivot on the pain, to act with love in the world, is truly revolutionary. The broken-hearted are the love revolutionaries on the planet at this time of reckoning. They know what matters because they have lost something really precious.

Even so, it is a moral wrong to leave the burden of addressing lovelessness and violence on the people, other animals, and Nature who are also impacted by injustice, who are also broken-hearted. The love revolution cannot progress without the people, businesses, and governments who cause harm, acquiescing to nonviolent appeals for justice and love. Everyone, to varying extents are adversely affected, perhaps they are even feeling heartache, when others are in pain and being treated unfairly.

These three ideas, if cherished deeply, can be the ethics that comprise the moral code for peace on Earth:

Love. Nonviolence. Eco justice.

With peace for all, there will be no broken-heartedness.

Love

A T THIS TIME in my life, I am holding onto one idea above all others. It is an idea that has become a belief that is unshakeable despite being put to the test on many occasions. I have an unshakeable belief in love. Love is at the heart of what I think is needed to address harm and loss of all kinds, for all kinds. Typically, love is understood as a feeling and, often, as a romantic connection in private between people. This matters, but for our purposes love is more of an action, often many actions, to make a difference for the better in our lives and the world. Love is as love does. If it does not look and feel loving for the most vulnerable and most oppressed, it is not love. To be able to believe in love, in the absence of love, is one of the hardest things in the world to do. To be nursing a broken heart from what I witnessed as a child, in my family and, later, in other families, and to try to be loving in the world, is also one of the hardest things to do.

Given this, I do not say the next point lightly. I think the love revolution, on many occasions, is happening with broken-hearted people who are expressing love out into the world. In so doing they are transforming their broken-heartedness into love energy instead of hate energy. This is one of the secrets of a broken heart, we can be experts in the importance of being loving. A gem of hope is that love that comes from broken-heartedness can be a gentle way to self-heal. And this love is a potentially revolutionary force outwards in the world. In the deepest, most hurt parts of ourselves, when love has been lost, or is not known, the smallest act of kindness to ourselves is extraordinary. This is the pivot point of hope in the world.

Before writing this book, I had come to a crossroad in my thinking about love. I felt that I needed to research more deeply what I meant by this cherished belief. This is because it was not self-evident what love might involve in many complex, conflictual, and violent situations. Nor is it self-evident how love can influence the powerful elites of society to take their proper responsibilities for harms and injustices done. I remember hooks writing that she came to theory as a young person to try to find a way to make the pain of racism go away.[1] She explains that for such a theory to have value we would need to work on making it help us know how to address the issue. This is because it is one thing to have a set of ideas and quite another to put them into practice. I really understood her in a way that I didn't with university textbooks. At a rational level, I understand that theories help us explain the world and guide us in knowing how to act. As a set of beliefs, assumptions, claims, and strategies, theories hold a promise for a better world. I have been almost totally relying on hooks' ideas about love for my own practice. But, this has become more and more inadequate for me as her ideas do not readily translate into my situation. Thus, I have arrived at a point where I want to acknowledge and build upon hooks' idea of the love ethic and develop a theory of love. Theory aims to make statements that can be considered by others for their verity and usefulness. Sociological theories are not trying to provide evidence or proof, as such, but they do need to ring true as feasible, believable and worthy of our attention. This chapter and the ones that follow outline some of my thinking about love which form the basis of a theory of love. A different understanding of love is needed to guide concerned citizens in responding to the heart-breaking justice issues of our times. Thus, I am looking for an expansive, multi-dimensional way of thinking about love to guide personal and planetary healing and justice work. I came to call this type of love *revolutionary love*.

The four letter word

It is perplexing that it took me a long time to come to have the courage to use the word love in my work. It was a serendipitous moment when I found the key that helped me link the idea of love to my professional practice. I was teaching in social work when a student gave me one of bell hooks' books. It happened very early on in my academic career, back in the 1990s. The book was called *Teaching to transgress: Education as the practice of freedom*.[1] In it, hooks writes that the classroom could be a revolutionary space where people could know democracy and know what it was like to be respected for their ideas. I found that truly radical because academia felt very controlled in what was expected of students, even though they were adult learners. This was my introduction to bell hooks. I have to thank that social work student from way back for passing me the book. It was one of those career defining moments. The idea of love has intrigued me ever since. I went on to do my doctorate on trying to understand love in an academic setting, and what that meant for my subsequent practice.

Here we are, fast forward more than twenty years later. Perhaps most clearly, in the last two years, I have become very focused on understanding everything that I do as being inspired by what hooks calls the love ethic. The love ethic, or ethic of love, is a bundle of values and capacities that inspires me, in the darkest of times, to pivot toward loving actions. hooks was a Black American woman who, during her lifetime, wrote more than forty books. She was a professor of English and travelled all over the world giving speeches and presentations and talking with people about issues of racism and how it impacts Black Americans. While hooks was writing from her own lived experience, and speaking predominantly to her own people, her ideas have value for everybody on the planet at this time. She was basically saying that love needs to be understood as more than our emotions, and more than sexualised ideas or intimacy between people. Rather, love is action in the world to uphold justice and wellbeing. hooks says that where there is love, there will be no violence, there will be no oppression.[2] She particularly anchored her analysis of what is not okay around issues of: white supremacy as the cause of racism; patriarchy as the cause of sexism, and; capitalism as the cause of class discrimination. hooks writes that there is a lack of love, or a culture of lovelessness — sometimes she calls it a culture of domination — that impacts minority status groups or undesirable groups of people.[2] I found this idea of practising love as a conscious political action appealing. The implication is we need to think of oppressive situations as the spaces and places where we can use love to work for justice.

Her book *All about love* is very inspirational.[3] If you have not read it yet, I encourage you to get hold of it. Even though it has been around a long time, I think it is a seminal piece of writing. hooks defines love as the combined forces of care, responsibility, knowledge, critical thinking, and compassion.[2] She says, to make the difference, these ideas and abilities need to be actions in the world. I agree with hooks that theory is meaningless unless we are going to make the commitment to use the ideas to take action. According to hooks, love is the answer to all types of oppression. While I find that may be a simplistic statement, I also find it expands my way of thinking about love. It gives us a sense of what we can do that might make a difference for the better in any situation. No matter how constraining, no matter how violent, no matter how devastating the circumstance we find ourselves in, we can think "What will be a loving action in this situation?" It is so courageous and, potentially, empowering to lead with love in such situations.

What love asks of us

One of the implications of hooks' idea of love is that there are a few layers to it. Firstly, we need to constantly practice self-love but not in a narcissistic way. Rather, by genuinely understanding self-love as being about caring for ourselves and healing from trauma. Secondly, self-love is needed so we can contribute to the world without reacting out of our trauma or wounding. Thirdly, we need to foster a willingness to love others, including other animals and Nature, as part of what love is about. What has been significant for me as a social worker, is that love requires me to stand with minority status groups and places being exploited or abused. Fourthly, love requires us, as well, to be willing to stand up and challenge the powerful, privileged people — the organisations, managers, governments, and big businesses. That is, to challenge the people who actually cause the inequalities in society that run along the fracture lines of oppression such as racism, classism, sexism, disablism, and speciesism.

The challenging of injustice needs to be undertaken with love. This involves peaceful, respectful dialogue and problem-solving with all parties, both those who are impacted by injustice and those who are complicit. People need to be held accountable. When our actions cause harm, we need to make amends, we need to take responsibility. This emphasis on responsibility is part of hooks' definition of love.[2] I really like that. One of the questions to ask for love to be realised is "Whose responsibility is it to do what is needed?" Closely followed by this question "How do you get powerful people, who may not see that they've caused harm, to take responsibility?" Freire says we need to bring people to the dialogue table.[4] To bring substantive outcomes for the oppressed people, the task is to work through the justice issue by listening and negotiating. We can't shy away from seeking dialogue with powerful people and organisations. Nor can we underestimate how hard it is to engage powerful people. Without them we cannot get very far with the justice and love work that needs to happen.

A commitment to self development is another aspect to hooks' definition of love, which she explains by drawing on Scott Peck's work, *The road less travelled*.[5] hooks describes love as a willingness to extend ourselves. That is, to be willing to learn for our personal growth. Further, love involves our ability and willingness to support others to extend themselves and learn for the good of others.[3] I really like that definition. This idea of love derives originally from Eric Fromm's seminal book, *The art of loving*.[6] Fromm explains that responsibility is a key aspect of love but that it could become a negative if responsibility is used to dominate others. Respect for others needs to be linked with responsibility because respect is about not exploiting and hurting others.[6] This brings us to the heart of the matter. We cannot just stand in judgement about what is going on. We have to come into a situation, take an ethical position guided by love and justice, and look to make a contribution where we are willing to learn as well.

For example, love would make us concerned about issues of race, racial inequality, systemic racism, however you think about it. We need to be willing to look at our own internal attitudes and beliefs. As a white woman, I need to make sure that I am not complicit with colonialism and white supremacy and what all of that means for minority social groups. I like hooks' definition of love as a political concept, not to take away from personal meanings of love and how that feels, but adding to and extending the personal idea of love. Love is action in the world to make a difference around matters of oppression. Freire notes that oppression is about overwhelming control and domesticating of peoples' thinking to uncritically accept unequal situations.[4] He sees dialogue between equals as love in action and writes that without love for the world, dialogue cannot be achieved.[4] In a similar vein to hooks, Freire explains how love is about courage, not fear, and involves a dedication to join with others to struggle for their liberation. They both warn against seeing love as sentimental or being duped by love as a pretext for exploitation. Love needs to lead to more acts of love otherwise it is something else courting the name of love.[4]

Love power as a counter to violence power

A particular moral conundrum arising from hooks' ideas is that love and violence are mutually exclusive. That is, where there is love there can be no violence. Both love and violence involve the exercise of power. However, in both instances, the power looks and feels very different and has very different goals and ethics. If there is abuse, exploitation and violence of any sort happening in a relationship, then hooks would say, that is not love. It may be the person being abusive says they love you, but the words and the actions do not align. I am reluctant to say that maybe there are not many people who have relationships where there is no violence and no exploitation. I believe that within every relationship it is possible to increase the amount of love and decrease, and remove, any violence and exploitation that is happening. So, I would not want to be quite as strident as hooks when she says where there is love there is no oppression. I think it can be much messier than that. People love each other in situations of violence. It does not make the violence morally okay. The two phenomena – love and violence – can co-exist, even though love would be deeply imprinted by the violence, as my personal experience highlights.

The places where love is most needed are places of violence. Belief in the power of love to overcome the power of violence is a very hard belief to hold on to. Certainly in my social work career, I have had to be willing, many times, to step into situations of extreme unsafety for myself and other people.

These were situations of injustice and violence. One example occurred in the situation I have mentioned relating the troubled relationship between Yarloop and Alcoa World Alumina at Wagerup in Western Australia.[7] On this particular occasion I had to respond to a community member's concern that one of their neighbours was going to blow up Alcoa's management offices. This was occurring in a very charged situation where the adverse impacts on the community were intensifying in the early 2000s.[8] The neighbour owned guns and was one of many residents who were distraught and outraged by what the mining company was doing to their town. Many also felt cheated with the payment for their property which they felt forced to sell due to pollution concerns. I supported the concerned person to stop his angry neighbour from responding to the injustices with violence. It was an unsafe situation for myself and others that risked becoming a criminal matter rather than a justice matter.

History has given us some remarkable examples of people who respond with love power in life threatening, violent situations. Love is needed to resist violence in the most oppressive of situations where the culture of domination is reinforced with extreme control and dehumanisation. Behrouz Boochani is a Kurdish journalist and writer who sought refuge as an asylum seeker in Australia. He was taken to an off-shore detention centre on Manus Island where he spent six years. As part of his resistance to the violence he experienced and witnessed towards others, he wrote *No friends but the mountain: Writing from Manus prison*.[9] He won several significant Australian book awards. *The Guardian* newspaper reported that his book was praised by award judges as a significant example of the power of witness and of writing as resistance.[10] He wrote the book in secret by sending small segments on WhatsApp to supporters in Australia. It remains a major indictment of the lovelessness and violence by the Federal Government. Boochani was not permitted to attend the book award ceremony in person and was subsequently given safe haven in New Zealand.

The Federal Government activated a previously unused part of the *Migration Act* 1958 to legitimate the off-shore detention of people seeking asylum. The Government acted in the name of protecting the national interests, presumably for the public good. Proponents of the harsh treatment of asylum seekers would consider their actions as morally right, even loving, in protecting Australians. The international convention on the right to seek asylum was transgressed and continues to be transgressed. The harm to asylum seekers is both unjust and morally unsound and highlights to me that what is done in the name of love of country is not necessarily an innocent idea or action.

A focus on power

Embedded in my arguments and reflections so far in this book, and often invisible as a direct phenomenon, is the idea of power. I am interested in love as a revolutionary force for good, hence the idea of revolutionary love. Another way of saying this is I am interested in love as a form of power. I believe love as power is able to resist, challenge, and change violence. So, I am bringing a focus onto power here, as part of holding myself and others accountable. For now, I need to be accountable for how my theorising is not power neutral or without effects in the world. For some people, the implications of a theory of love are unwelcome and even threatening. Thus, we come to the recognition that power is as complex to describe and understand as the idea of love. Steven Lukes explains this is because power is always value-dependent.[11] This means how power is exercised is related to how power is understood and who is doing the acting.

Power has been defined in a myriad of ways. Many definitions have in common the point that power involves some amount of influence. This influence can include force being used against people and other beings. Max Weber identified three types of power: traditional, charismatic, and rational-legal.[12] Traditional power is located in people on the basis of social conventions, such as the Prime Minister or the Pope. Charismatic power is located in an individual's personality and elicits followers, such as social influencers on digital media. Rational-legal authority is not possessed by an individual per se, but is located in the role they occupy and often underpinned by legislation. For example, the *Migration Act* 1958 authorises the Australian navy to intercept asylum seekers and take them to an off-shore detention centre.

Power can also be operating in a situation as an implicit or direct threat of harmful consequences if certain behaviours occur, or do not occur. Power is always present in any interaction from the intimate personal realm to the public realm.[13] All actions and nonactions are imbued with power. Discourses are the collectivity of ways that people communicate, interact, and make meaning in specific historical and material circumstances. Discourse is usually mentioned in terms of dominant discourses which serve to normalise the ideas of the elites of society as the truth to be followed. This is how the power to influence, achieve goals, and certain outcomes are closely tied to how knowledge is understood and used. C. W. Mills claimed that most people adapt to modern life shaped by governments, corporations, and the military.[14] The elites have more resources to employ to promote knowledge and ideas that serve their purposes. Michel Foucault described these resources as mechanisms of control and surveillance in places such as prisons and mental hospitals.[15] The aim is the use of power, what Foucault calls disciplinary power, to gain the compliance of undesirable social groups who are regarded as being of less value or who are threatening to the power elites.

Foucault's treatise on power attempts to challenge the idea that power is a zero-sum phenomenon, where someone, or an entity, has 'it' and others do not have it. At the same time, this is not to deny that, for someone who is experiencing domination and violence, it can feel like they have no power. This in itself is part of the dominant discourse that can keep people feeling fatalistic and defeated, entrapped in what Foucault calls "docile bodies".[13] Foucault argues that power exists in the everyday interactions between people as well as in the social and other institutions of society.[13] Smith refers to the indirect forms of power as "extra local relations of ruling".[16] This explains how power is layered throughout society and is far from a benign force in unequal societies and relationships. Whenever power is considered, it also needs to be tied to the possibility of resistance to the exercise of power.[13] Against terrible odds, Boochani resisted the surveillance and control of the elites in Canberra and the managers of the off-shore detention centre. He resisted first of all by surviving and then by writing a protest book of historical significance.

A theory of love has to be relevant to guide responses to experiences such as Boochani's imprisonment and all other situations of violence and oppression. If love is the answer, its form is far from clear. When its absence is related to violence and injustice, it is a very troubling moral challenge that needs to be addressed by a society. As Gandhi said, the moral fibre of a society is to be judged by the quality of life of its most vulnerable members. Issues of lovelessness, violence, and injustice are issues related to how power is used, or not used, by powerful people and organisations. Power is the antithesis of love when it is used (or withheld) and the impact is harm, trauma, even death.

When the Federal Government legislated the *Border Force Act* 2015, it was attempting to silence concerned workers who were bearing witness to the human suffering on Manus Island and other off-shore detention centres. The legal threat was that people speaking out would be breaking the law and dealt with under the provisions of the Act. Doctors for Refugees resisted this threat and spoke out against the Act, arguing for the right of detainees to receive medical care.[17] The Government did not invoke the Act against them and subsequently removed that stricture for many, but not all, professions. Social workers remain legally unable to speak out about what they might witness in off-shore detention centres. Immoral legislation needs to be resisted and doing so can be successful. Resistance against harmful use of power is a form of love as long as it is nonviolent.

My unloving use of power

As a social worker, it took me too many years to understand that having goodwill towards people in client situations was not sufficient to ensure the best outcome possible for them. I saw myself as a good person but failed to appreciate the authority I wielded in my professional role. I also did not give sufficient credence to how people seeking help would perceive my role, for example, in public mental health services. I was aware of the stigma of mental illness thanks to Goffman's book *Stigma: Notes on the management of spoiled identity*.[18] And I held doggedly onto a fragment of an idea from Szasz's book that mental illness is a myth.[19] But I did not take this further to place myself in the picture. I was part of the state apparatus of controlling certain groups of people. This control was often against their will, leaving many people worse off after state intervention. Only now, as I am writing this book, did I go back to Szasz to find a quote that I needed to heed in my practice. He wrote that institutionalised forms of helping and diagnosing can become an enslavement of the patient.[19] This enslavement can occur with little gain of knowledge or responsibility by the patient or the helper.[19] I was naive about power yet I used it in ways that were unloving towards others, with few negative repercussions for myself.

It starts with self-love

Love is a form of power. This is an unusual way of thinking about power because power is usually thought of as a negative matter. Love as a form of power can help bring a focus to how power can be a positive force for good in the world. Love can be about self-love, love of other people, love of other animals, and love of Nature. It needs to be cultivated and practised in relationships of all kinds. Thich Nhat Hanh taught that, according to the Buddhist tradition, true love involves the four aspects of loving, namely kindness, compassion, joy, and freedom.[20] These capacities are to be practised in our relationships with the people in our daily lives but require the practice of love of self at the same time. Hanh gives guidance on how to restore peace within ourselves when troubled or hurt by another person, how to overcome pride that can be a barrier to loving communication, and what is needed to care for (heal) our pain.[20] The message is clear: we cannot love others if we are overloaded with pain, hurt, and resentments to the point of being hopeless, helpless, and feeling unloved. Hanh says this is because true love is "being there"[20] for another which requires knowing how to be there for ourselves as well. He believes that giving our presence to others is the most precious gift of all.[20]

I feel the need to respectfully place a qualifying statement alongside Hanh's ideas. Love as a type of power is enacted in a social context. Where there is violence and inequality, love can be a dangerous experience for many people. To be present with an abusive person is not something that would be safe, or even warranted, as a first action.[21] Inequality, and the resultant violence, needs to be held central in any theorising about love. hooks writes extensively to Black Americans about the issue of self-hate which she links directly to internalised oppression due to racism and white supremacy.[3] She regards loving blackness in a racist world as an act of resistance.[22] She calls on Black people to love themselves rightly, aware that racism is a form of assault that leaves deep emotional wounds.[3] Additionally, there are different orders, or levels, of who is responsible to act and address harm. hooks would argue that powerful white supremacists have the highest order of responsibility to address racism. The level of responsibility for the disadvantaged or harmed parties is to keep acting to overcome harm from violence and injustice through self-love. This needs to include avoiding being dehumanised by developing a critical understanding of the situation.[4]

Love as self-care and care of others

I am interested in self-love in terms of caring for ourselves, being kind and gentle with ourselves, and doing the healing work related to our own wounds and trauma. This can be understood as self-empowerment, or power being exercised at the personal level. At the same time, it needs to be recognised that in an unequal world, members of disadvantaged and stigmatised social groups carry an unfair burden in the caring and healing work.[23] This caring work can go unrecognised and is not counted as part of the economic worth of a society. It is a dimension of sexism against women that they tend to provide most of the informal caring in families and communities. In professional situations, self-love is not the language used. Rather, it is talked about as self-care which is needed to enable practitioners to have the capacity to build rapport and have empathy for the people they engage with. It is well recognised that experiences such as vicarious trauma or compassion fatigue can occur from witnessing other peoples' distress.[24] In terms of workplace health and safety legislation, it is the responsibility of the practitioner as well as their workplace to ensure worker wellbeing so they are fit for work.[25] Thompson notes, however, that there can be a failure of legal duty of care responsibilities by management for practitioners who are experiencing, what he calls, "occupational stress".[26] The individual practitioner can be blamed for the stress issue and the broader workplace culture and resource factors are not considered. Individual attempts at self-care are diluted by toxic workplaces, or what Bloom refers to as "trauma-organising workplaces".[27] This might make the idea of self-care complicated and may take it beyond the realms of the self in self-care. It is important to view personal behaviours in their sociocultural context. Among other things, this can help us recognise why it might be so hard to maintain personal health, safety, and wellbeing in some situations.

It matters how we act in private places. It matters how we act in public places. We need to be congruent at home and at work. Violence can hide in the incongruence between our values and actions. We are starved for good examples of people in public spaces standing up and being accountable for their actions when harm is done. This contrasts with people without public profiles often stepping up to be counted and try to make the powerful accountable which can come at a high cost to themselves. We need to start with ourselves, to go gentle on ourselves. Then we can have the resilience and sustain ourselves for challenging the powerful. Again, this challenging needs to be done with love. I think that part of both Thich Nhat Hanh's legacy and bell hooks' legacy was that they were striving to live these ideas about love that they were writing about. They wanted to make a loving contribution in the world by starting with themselves and moving outwards to all the people with whom they had contact or influence. Thich Nhat Hanh travelled to western countries and lobbied prime ministers and presidents to stop their involvement in the war in his home country of Vietnam. He did this with love despite the pain of witnessing the suffering of his people.

The idea of eco-anxiety highlights for many of us, possibly most of us, that we are ongoingly witnessing injustices and harm. This concern for what is happening on the planet on so many levels is heart-breaking and can cause trauma. It can cause paralysis and can result in us losing hope of a better world. It can also have the effect of us not being so gentle, loving, and kind to ourselves. Deep ecologist Joanna Macy says we need to do our despair work by befriending our grief.[28] This may help us avoid seeing our despair as a pathology and, with this befriending of grief, be better able to contribute to planetary healing work.[29] Self-care and self-love can be regarded as parallel dimensions necessary for our commitment to being a love revolutionary. We need to care for and heal ourselves, to love ourselves, in the darkest of times. Otherwise our ability to stand beside and be with others of all species, of all kinds, all our Kin, will be limited and unsustainable in the long run.[30]

Love as justice work

A commitment to love necessarily extends us to a concern about justice. Of course, justice work is a long haul project with many, many actors contributing across the lifespan of the struggle. Think about the Black Lives Matter movement as one example. This term has recently been given to the contemporary nature of civil rights struggles by the racially oppressed and their allies which

have spanned decades and different countries.[31] I think hooks'
writing remains relevant in the Black Lives Matter movement.[32]
Its revolutionary potential arises from her willingness to put the
word love into a form that links the personal and the political.
It is a contested word in Western cultures. Even so, hooks puts
it right there in the middle of public life and issues. Her close
friend Cornel West, who is also significant in the Black Lives
Matter movement, says that "love is what justice looks like in
public".[33] I find that a very inspiring way to think about love.
Whether it is in public or in private, love is any action that avoids
being retaliatory and avoids harming others. Love is any action
that turns from violence, or neglect of people and other beings,
toward love. Love is the answer to experiences of lovelessness.
Love can heal broken hearts.

A cautionary note

A reading of my theory of love at this formative level of
development perhaps raises more questions than it answers.
Love is a highly valued idea and experience. It is equally highly
contested. Fromm recognised this when, in 1956, he wrote that
most people think of love as a pleasant sentiment or something
that we fall into.[6] Many people regard being loved as the most
important thing in life. Fromm argues that love is something
to be practised as a form of art, that it requires knowledge and
skills to build our capacity for love and to be loving.[6]

Laurie and Stark outline the main sociological critiques of the
idea of love which serve as a cautionary note in what is asked of
a theory of love. They identify three critiques, where love: could
result in heteronormative social relations and, thus, annihilate

differences and deepen inequalities; that love is a derivative of desire and, thus, not a primary concept in its own right; and that love is not amenable to empirical study and must be rejected.[34] I think each of these critiques has merit but I want to bring my attention to the first point which is most relevant. The authors are saying we need to guard against moralising in relation to love which condones love as acceptable only in some types of relationships. Namely, there are limitations to a theory of love that sets up dualisms of who is valued and free to love who is not valued and not free to love. Such strictures undercut the moral principles that all beings are equal and that all beings are worthy of love. At the same time, this risk should not be used to avoid recognising the human causes of the material realities of oppression. In addressing the human causes, the responsible parties should be afforded equal moral regard while being held accountable. Not an easy political or moral position to uphold. Moral pressure by nonviolent advocates for justice may be unwelcome for the responsible powerful parties. But it is not the same as violence against the powerless parties in the justice issue.

I also want to avoid extreme relativism where any behaviour in the name of love is morally acceptable. It may be the case that isms such as fascism, colonialism, capitalism, and the social expressions of these – authoritarianism, racism, classism, sexism, speciesism – involve attachment to certain ideas of the public good, of what is for the good of society, as being expressions of love. Supporters of capitalism would want to argue, as just one example, that the pursuit of profits by mining natural resources is a good thing for society. In Australia, various state mines acts and the *Federal Corporations Act* 2001 make it legal to do this.

Therefore, mining can be considered as a form of moral good and an expression of love in a capitalist society. This line of argument about what constitutes love is not one I can agree with. Love as working for democracy based on sustainable, socialist ideas is more compatible in terms of my overarching political stance. But democracy, too, is a fraught idea and far from a realised project.[35] Nevertheless, I will keep de-linking capitalism and all the other isms from my understanding of love. I will keep valuing a form of active, participatory democracy that protects and values diversity within a moral code of love, justice, sustainability and peace.

Part of what is required to grapple with the issue of the idealising of love are other capacities such as critical thinking and analysis. These capacities enable us to place love as a political practice in its social, historical and economic contexts. In so doing, an appreciation of the unequal material consequences of how the elites construct the public good and where love fits can be achieved. This is supported by Laurie and Stark who present the argument that love is not only a matter of moral consideration, but also needs to be understood as being part of the material processes of life.[34] They believe a theory of love should explain why love sometimes leads to fascism and, at other times, leads to communism. They claim a political love must break down and overthrow norms and institutions and, hence, act as a revolutionary force.[34]

In terms of what is involved in being a love revolutionary, I am not sure the task is to radically break the existing social structures — the 'storming of the Bastille' idea of revolution. But I also do not wish to be complicit with social changes that are indolent (e.g. the equality gap for Australian First Nation People) or even regressive (e.g. the silencing of abuse in off-shore detention centres with the *Border Protection Act* 2015) or not even on the public agenda as requiring attention (e.g. torturous treatment of mental patients in seclusion).[36, 37]

I agree with Laurie and Stark's suggestion that we need to embrace difference, complexity, and conflict of values, including ideas about love.[34] This involves resisting the homogenising of others' views. It also involves resisting attempts at unifying social structures in the name of love at the expense of injustices that might thereby be concealed and silenced.

Love practices

Love is a big idea that inspires a broad range of actions and strategies for the highest possible good in a situation. Listening is an act of love. Caring for someone who is hurting is an act of love. Putting out a helping hand to someone is an act of love. Befriending a lonely person is loving. Ensuring animals are treated fairly is loving. Removing invasive plants from an ecosystem is an act of love. Taking responsibility for harm caused is love. Problem-solving issues as diverse as: a lack of housing, loss of employment, unsafe neighbourhoods, unfair business practices, culling of unwanted wild animals, and pollution of rivers and waterways, are all acts of love. If any of these opportunities for love involve unfairness or violence, a different order of love practices is needed. Love as a power-sensitive approach is a political practice that seeks to address harm of all kinds for all kinds.

Loving practices towards others need to meet, match, and overcome violence and injustice. Love power focussed on addressing harm has the hallmarks of concerned people challenging dominating people and places. This challenging needs to be done with love, not with violence, hatred or revenge. Challenging with love means we have to love the dominating people and places even as we advocate for the oppressed and hurt. Love practices are not about capitulating or naively cooperating actions. It can take a lot of courage and wisdom to know what to do in a specific situation where love is lacking. And even then, no amount of courage and wisdom may be enough to shift the views and actions of dominant groups. Challenging with love is far from easy but lovelessness can only be overcome with love and all that love makes possible. Using violence to overcome lovelessness inverts the dominance hierarchy. The pecking order of inequality remains. Violence is reinforced as the means of addressing violence. In turn, belief in the power of love is diminished.

If challenging with love does not succeed in enabling justice for those experiencing violence and lovelessness, then these harms must be resisted. The resistance against harm needs to be done with love. It is not always possible to bring about change for the better. It may be a long time coming. Meanwhile minority status groups and their advocates need to refuse to become violent or to accede to the dominant groups' regressive ideas and control. Resistance takes many forms as contemporary social and environment movements show. Nonviolent direct actions are the core skills for challenging and resisting dominance and violence. They become more potent when the struggles for justice take on mass scale protests and include impacted groups. Resistance also needs to be undertaken with love because the way to love and peace is through love and peace. In unsafe situations at work or at home, knowing how to survive while keeping your integrity and not betraying your own values is sometimes all you have to hold on to. Berhoux Boochani showed us this.

The aim of love practices is to address the violence and injustice in a situation. Love practitioners cannot witness harm and heartbreak and do nothing. They seek change which also needs to occur with love. When love practices engage the powerful in dialogue, then change becomes possible. This justice work involves changes to unfair legislation such as mental health acts that authorise the use of seclusion and restraint against mental patients. Love practices seek changes to unsafe organisational workplaces where authoritarianism and inadequate support of staff cause horizontal and vertical violence. Love addresses lovelessness. Thus, the third main skill of loving practices is changing with love. Sometimes, it is the advocates of change who need to model the change themselves. Leaders of social change efforts need to be loving and fair in how they treat their people and those they are asking to change. Change of legislation, systems, social norms, and powerful peoples' views can take a long time. Resisting and challenging with love needs to be maintained to keep moral pressure on the powerful groups. If done with love, where they are listened to and respectfully negotiated with, success is more likely. And retaliation and increasing violence may be minimised.

Nonviolence

Nonviolence as love in action

It follows from hooks' ideas that love refers to a range of capacities, and yet underpinning all these capacities, it is synonymous with nonviolence. Mahatma Gandhi's idea of love is also closely related to nonviolence. I have found his idea of Satyagraha, or truth force, to be inspiring. Gandhi developed his ideas during India's nonviolent independence struggle from British occupation. There have been many books, and even movies, made about his life and work.[1] Gandhi maintained a detailed diary which scholars and activists have drawn on to guide their own thinking and activism.[2, 3] India gained independence in 1947 after many decades of struggle and hardship for its people. Gandhi is revered because of how he tried to model his belief in nonviolence as a means of struggle against what he saw as the oppressive forces of the British Empire. Nevertheless, he has been criticised for being racist and sexist in early adulthood.[4] He changed his attitudes and behaviours by holding himself to the same high moral demands he asked of the people in power in India. Gandhi developed a form of civil disobedience by drawing on the Buddhist concept of Ahimsa, meaning love, and Satyagraha, meaning nonviolence. He saw love as a way of life that we need to consciously practise at every opportunity and nonviolence as a method of struggle.[5] Gandhi explained that 'satya' means truth and 'agraha' means polite insistence or holding firmly to, where the combination of terms refers to truth force.[6]

In 1909, Gandhi said that his imprisonment as a young lawyer in South Africa during uprisings against apartheid was his path to God. He believed practising restraint and gentleness in the face of abuse was important.[5] This is the key principle of meeting violence with nonviolent resistance and self-discipline and refusing to resort to violence. Gandhi was clear that violence only leads to more violence. He wrote at the time that war demoralises and brutalises people. War goes against every good moral canon. War is about lust and murder, and, as such, is not the way to independence.[5] Gandhi said there could be no love if compassion, forgiveness, and equality were absent.[6] Gandhi saw nonviolence as a positive power despite the 'non' in the term. Therefore, we need both love, Ahimsa, and nonviolence, Satyagraha.

Drawing upon Ghandi, nonviolence, as I understand it, refers to the peaceful, respectful, and tactical use of power and influence. The aim is to pressure high power individuals and groups to uphold protesters' justice claims. It can include a broad range of nonviolent direct action strategies such as street marches, media campaigns, petitions, sit-ins, and civil disobedience.[7] Chenoweth looked at all the major uprisings and revolutions of recent history. She found that the most successful – the ones that could endure through all sorts of challenges to achieve the public's claims for justice – were ones that were not violent.[8] I think that is intriguing and gives us hope that we can trust in the power of nonviolence.

Martin Luther King Jr's philosophy of civil disobedience was strongly influenced by Gandhi's ideas on love as nonviolence. King often said that he learned his faith from God, and lived by nonviolence principles from Gandhi.[9] For example, some of the nonviolence principles King practised are: nonviolence is a way of life for courageous people; it seeks to win friendship and understanding; nonviolence chooses love instead of hate, and; nonviolence believes that the universe is on the side of justice.[9]

Nonviolence situates love as reaching for the highest good, as hooks says, in ourselves and the other person.[10] Linked to this, Gandhi said that nonviolence refers to ways of struggling for justice and good in the world, without doing harm to the oppressed or resorting to violence.[6] Many of the helping professions talk about nonmaleficence, which means doing no harm.[11] This compares with beneficence, which means doing good and acting in the best interests of the person. I really like the concept of nonmaleficence. It serves as another way of thinking about nonviolence. The intention is to consciously aim to be of value and service to people in formal, professional helping relationships, but also, more generally, in our personal lives.

Trauma as evidence of violence

I think the idea of trauma helps us to translate what the experience of violence can look and feel like across multiple situations. Bloom explains that trauma is about the harm caused by unwelcome experiences such as violence and unfair treatment.[12] What is really helpful in how Bloom perceives trauma is that it aligns with our experiences in our bodies. And in turn, how that can then affect our hearts, our ability to love, and our ability to flourish in the world. Bloom was a psychiatrist in a mental health ward in Philadelphia in the 1980s. On the basis of her practice experiences, she developed a program called *The Sanctuary Model* with two colleagues.[13] Bloom was trying to understand the parallels that can happen in systems of care for people receiving mental health treatment and what was happening in an individual person's life. Bloom has been influential in shaping the trauma-informed care approach to mental health conditions. This approach acknowledges peoples' experiences of distress, and offers help that enables healing and recovery, and does not further add to their trauma.

One of Bloom's most important ideas used for unpacking what trauma looks like is how trauma involves the lack of safety being experienced by the person. Unsafety becomes a potential indicator of harm and possibly trauma. I am concerned about particular types of trauma where there has been an injustice or harm done to somebody. Bloom identifies four types of safety needed for trauma-informed responses with people we may have contact with and for responding to our own trauma. The four types of safety are: physical safety; psychological safety; social safety; and moral safety.[12] She says we need to cultivate a sense of physical safety in ourselves so that we feel secure, not only in our bodies, but also financially. Further, physical safety means we are free from all types of violence, including self-destructive behaviour where we are violent toward ourselves. Psychological safety is the second type of safety, which refers to being able to undertake self-care and self-discipline. It involves fostering our own self-esteem and the ability to live in a self-reflective way as part of a healthy, productive life. Social safety is the third type of safety that Bloom says is important in avoiding trauma and knowing how to begin the recovery process. This refers to the ability to interact with others without being compromised or harmed, or without harming others. The idea of social safety links to the fourth type of safety, moral safety. It can be said that moral safety exists when all the people in a situation freely follow a set of values and commitments that are consistent with treating people respectfully. Moral safety involves being able to act according to our values. Bloom writes that moral unsafety is experienced when a person has lost the sense of justice. This sense of the world being just is central to healing and recovering from trauma and violence.[12] Moral unsafety occurs when a person has been devalued by someone with authority over them. The loss of belief in the world being fair can undermine a belief in love as a positive power in healing and wellbeing.

I find these four types of safety to be helpful because, when considering them, we could perhaps identify ways we do not feel safe. From this, we can track the reason for this experience of unsafety and begin to address it. Violence can be understood as the threat or experience of unsafety in one or more ways. It can be about unsafety, not only for an individual, but for a whole group of people or other animals. There is another related idea that I find helpful in deepening what it might feel like to experience unsafety involving violence. This is the idea of autonomy infringement, which was coined by Hem and colleagues.[14] They say that unsafety can occur if the person feels some sort of intrusion – usually unwelcome and unwarranted – on their sense of self and their autonomy in the world. It could involve coercion and all types of violence, and is quite a complicated area in some aspects. As a general ethical statement, I want to suggest that there are types of violence that cause autonomy infringement that is experienced as unsafety and trauma. This is not to say it will be clear what needs to be done to address the unsafety. The answer, however, must involve nonviolence.

Trauma exists on a continuum of harm and experiences of unsafety. Trauma can become stored in a person's memory and body, and significantly impact their relationships. It can be quite complex trauma, with the potential to compound over time into what is called intergenerational trauma. The Australian Human Rights Commission's *Bringing them home* report identified that First Nation children, who had been forcibly removed from their families, experienced trauma.[15] This government intervention was recognised by the Human Rights Commission as an attempt at genocide of an entire race, causing complex and intergenerational impacts ever since.[16] This is a deeply troubling example of how trauma influences life chances, and may impact peoples' ability to have safe and loving relationships. When the trauma is caused by systemic racism, it can lock whole social groups into survival struggles in situations not of their choosing.

With these points in mind, it is very concerning to me, as a member of the social work profession, that social work was directly implicated in the forced removal of First Nation children. The Australian Association of Social Workers has formally apologised for this travesty of justice. Yet it remains the case that First Nation children in Australia continue to be removed from their families. Some sources argue the removals are occurring at a higher rate than during what was called the

Stolen Generation.[17] It is a pressing matter of national concern, and for social work as a profession, to work with First Nation People to change the systemic issues that keep perpetuating racism despite many good-hearted people working in these systems.[18]

An example of moral unsafety

As a social worker for many decades now, there have been an unknown number of times when I have been in situations where I have acted in a way that was inconsistent with my values. It is hard to write about because it is such a large area of moral injury. Perhaps the most concerning example would be when I worked in the mental health system as a clinical social worker. As I have mentioned, with the authority of the *Mental Health Act*, I had the legal power, along with others, to force some people to have a mental health assessment. Sometimes I was also part of decisions where treatment was enforced against their wishes. This was the most troubling and disturbing experience of my life. My ability to keep living with a sense of integrity was seriously compromised. It makes me aware that when any of us are party to behaviours that put us out of step with our deep values, it is not something that has a quick or satisfactory answer. However, we do need to take our appropriate responsibilities for harmful actions, even if there is no specific evidence to hand at the time of the harm being done to others.

Nonviolence is my number one value, and yet I was complicit with what is legal violence in the mental health context.[19] I believe forced treatment is unethical violence toward others. In fact, I see all violence as unethical. Even if my actions are seen to be necessary at that point in time to keep the person safe – it becomes a morally troubling circumstance to say the least. There have been strong critiques of mental health practitioners by activists in the mental health lived experience movement and Mad Studies, which I am not immune to. A valuable book in this regard is *Searching for a rose garden: Challenging psychiatry, fostering mad studies*, edited by Jasna Russo and Angela Sweeney.[20]

Violence, and all the forms of oppression that go with it, really threatens peoples' ability to experience love. Violence also threatens peoples' capacity for the love needed in justice struggles. I have built on the idea of broken-heartedness by considering the trauma that is experienced through all sorts of unsafety, namely psychological, social, emotional, and moral unsafety. Actions that foster safety are potentially ways to practise nonviolence in our relationships with others and with ourselves. It is also where I see that justice work can become hard to undertake. This is because of the impact of broken-heartedness on the very people who are experiencing injustice and trauma. At the same time, they are often the very same people who stand up and are at the front of justice struggles.

The ability to act with moral safety and congruence when in a position with legal authority over others is a major challenge in contemporary human services. There are many troubling politics that come with a commitment to be loving and nonviolent in contexts that are often loveless and violent.

About more-than-human trauma

Another note I would like to make here is, when we talk about violence and harm, we tend to mostly think about violence and harm in relation to people. This is understandable. But it is indicative of anthropocentrism, which is an exclusive focus on humans and a privileging of human interests at the cost of other species. The idea of anthropocentric harm draws us to be aware of the violence committed against other animals and Nature.[21] It is an important idea for describing how human-centeredness causes speciesism. This bias against other species can stop us from upholding the principles of the equal intrinsic worth of all sentient beings. As part of challenging anthropocentrism, the idea of more-than-human brings attention to other beings and entities who also experience loss and trauma. The more-than-human refers to the complexities of entanglements and interconnections across species and beings.[22] It is premised in an ecological world view that asks of humans that we seek eco justice for all our Kin.

Humans need to practice nonmaleficence towards other animals as a commitment to nonviolence. However, as Alger explains, there is an industrialised and globalised approach to the farming of some animal species for human consumption.[23] In her book *Five essays for freedom*, Alger writes that the normalised use of other animals allows business owners to make money on a scale that is difficult to comprehend.[23] As a society, we do not give sufficient credence to the harm and suffering of the animals, and the trauma they experience. As part of this, I do not believe you can have humane killing on that kind of scale. I think it is commercialised killing for human gain. I am extremely concerned about the scale of violence toward certain groups of other animals. I believe that peace will not be known on the planet while we continue to kill, and use other animals, in these ways. They experience pain and trauma often associated with their death, but also due to other uses such as research and entertainment.

Nonviolence and other animals

Violence and injustices of all kinds are indicators of lovelessness. If you love somebody, you do not hurt them or treat them unfairly. When I think about the lovelessness that occurs between humans it is truly heart-breaking. At the same time, everyday there are reminders of the travesties of justice and extreme violence done to other animals. If you love somebody, you do not eat them. There is an undeclared, sanitised, and legitimated war on other animals, especially animals farmed for human consumption. There are troubling intersections between colonialism, capitalism, and patriarchy, and how these forms of social and economic systems cause disadvantage and injustice. Speciesism is part of this broader societal hierarchy of who is important and who can be eaten. Intricately causal in this state of unfairness is the fact that the use of other animals is profitable. In a capitalist society, monetary gain tends to sit in a tight tension with moral considerations for sentient beings. However, if enough people stopped eating farmed animals, the profits would decline and the meat industry would have to diversify. Many businesses are already doing so as the consumption of some types of animal flesh are not as in-demand as they used to be.

I think the scale of suffering by other animals is so troubling that it cannot be excused morally. An economics of other animals mattering is needed. My multispecies ethics has been influenced by two key authors: Peter Singer's *Animal liberation* and Gary Franciones' writings, including his most recent book *Why veganism matters*. Bioethicist Peter Singer argues that our responsibility involves not only how we act but also how we might fail to act. Failing to act, directly or indirectly, adds to strangers' and other animals' suffering and therefore becomes a moral issue.[24] I agree with him when he explains how other animals are beings capable of feeling pain, and, therefore, they too should be afforded the concern and protection of society. Singer's book is recognised as the singularly important source of inspiration that activated the animal liberation movement in the 1970s. I read the book in my early twenties and it shifted my view of the world. It caused me to better understand the malaise I felt growing up about how animals were treated as commodities and less important than people. I re-read some of Singer's writing recently and found the ethical premises for his call for animal liberation. He explains that suffering by any sentient being is grounds for considering them as worthy of moral regard and care. Singer believes that the being's characteristics are not what is important, rather that they have a right to live free of human exploitation.[24]

Singer claims animal liberation is about treating all species equally.[24] That they should have the same rights as humans. Singer makes an insightful point that I have held on tightly to ever since. Equality is not necessarily about equal treatment, rather it is about equal consideration.[24] Different treatment would not mean that it is acceptable to kill other animals for human consumption. Rather, it would mean that humans need to recognise the autonomy and right to be of other animals. Singer explains a little later that equality is a moral idea, not an assertion of fact.[24] This means other species' right to equal consideration will need to be struggled for in an unequal, speciesist society as it will not be readily accepted as a matter of equality.

I think Francione's purist vegan view that there is no grey area in the use of other animals is idealistic. He argues that any use of animals is unethical. Nevertheless, I do find his willingness to propound his views so strongly on behalf of other animals very inspiring. The idea that most stands out for me is that veganism is the moral baseline we need to live by.[25] His new book argues that it is a matter of justice as well as a moral priority to stop eating and using other animals for human benefit.[26] In a similar way to Singer, Francione argues that on the basis that other animals are sentient beings, not things, they should be considered to have personhood status. In turn, this means humans have moral obligations towards them. I find myself agreeing whole-heartedly, but a major shift in societal values is needed to stem the tide of speciesism that results in humans not regarding some other animals as moral beings.

Nonviolence practices

Acts of love are the building blocks of nonviolence practices. Nonviolence practices are communications and actions based on respect, kindness, nonforcing, willingness to listen, treating others as equals, and taking responsibility for harm done. These practices need safe and loving spaces and relationships to flourish. Another tier of practices is required where there is violence and injustice. These higher tier practices are challenging with love, resisting with love, and changing with love. Collectively, they are groupings of skills and processes that are premised on the ethic of nonviolence. This capacity of nonviolence is more than not being violent, although this absolutely has to be so. Nonviolence is a proactive, critically analysed practice that uses love power to address violence power. The critical analysis of abuse of power – for example by a NUM in a mental health ward – will illuminate how an authoritarian management structure causes unsafe workplaces where staff get bullied and scapegoated. A loving critical analysis will resist blaming the NUM or any one person and see the whole system level of the violence. As such, everyone who works in the system has some order of responsibility, including the NUM. Nonviolence practice avoids shaming and stigmatising people. Rather, people are invited, encouraged, and enabled to be responsible for their actions and inactions where harm has occurred. Nonviolence also recognises the harm caused by negative judgements of already devalued and traumatised social groups, with mental health patients being prime examples. Educating people with mental illness in stigma resistance strategies is a crucial example of nonviolence. This is because it will help people to avoid harm and understand the social and political factors that are contributing to feeling stigmatised.

Thus, trauma-informed care, and fostering trauma-informed systems of care, are possible due to a commitment to nonviolence. Doing no harm has to be valued as highly as doing good care. From these baseline principles, trauma-informed and trauma-reducing care can be provided. When care is about care, then nonviolence occurs. Love will be present and people will be treated fairly. Trauma-informed systems address horizontal violence between staff and vertical violence against clients. Good care is undermined when harm is not addressed in human services.

Unless nonviolence is promoted and modelled by management, the overall system will be a violence-prone place. In such circumstances, staff and clients are likely to experience violence. The proneness to violence is most apparent when the opposite to nonviolence is considered. Seclusion and restraint practices against mental patients are the extreme opposite of nonviolence. These actions in care services cause dehumanisation in the name of care. Nonviolence will show as substantial efforts being made to create safe places and sanctuaries for people needing care when grappling with mental health challenges. Nonviolence will show as legislation that does not require the use of violence, and governments actively challenging societal prejudices against minority status groups of all kinds.

Nonviolence will be a big part of care practices when patients feel respected, safe, and listened to as equal partners in the care being offered. Force will no longer be entwined in the caregiving. Staff will no longer bully or be bullied, scapegoat or be scapegoated. Nor will they be subjected to other forms of organisational violence. Distressed people will no longer be placed in seclusion rooms on their own. As a result, there will be less violence in the ward environment. Caring practitioners will be with them, offering comfort and tending to their needs. Trauma responses and acting out behaviours will be met with gentle, loving kindness.

The way forward is in the hands and hearts of people who are nonviolent in how they do their jobs and live their lives. The way forward is also in the hands and hearts of people who have known violence or themselves have been violent, and who turn towards nonviolence in order to break the cycle of violence. Nonviolence at home creates families who know how to keep each other safe. Children grow up knowing that nonviolence is closely linked to love and feeling fairly treated. Adults from loving, safe, and just families become workers who are loving, safe and fair to other workers and clients. In such homes and workplaces, people would be healthier, happier, and more able to help others. Nonviolence requires an ongoing commitment to learn about love where love is not entwined with violence. It also requires a commitment to practise love as nonviolence at home, at work, with other animals, and with Nature.

Eco Justice

Love is required for justice to matter

Justice matters because we love others. When we love others we want them to be treated fairly. Wherever there is violence or lovelessness, there is an issue of justice. A justice issue occurs when someone, a group, a community, or a species has been harmed, or their rights to peaceful co-existence have been intruded upon. Eco justice – or ecological justice – is an umbrella term for three interlinked types of justice: social justice for people; species justice for other animals, and; environmental justice for Nature. I will explain these types of justice and explore their interlinks to put the case for a more inclusive understanding of justice. This is important to ensure a theory of love encompasses all of life and the complex challenges related to sustaining life, peace, and wellbeing for all.

Justice for people

Typically, ideas of justice assume we are referring to justice for only humans. The term social justice is used to emphasise the social factors involved in justice issues. Social justice is needed when power differentials become unfair due to people of privileged status gaining at the expense of people in minority status groups. Social justice is the main value of the social work profession and is usually defined in terms of what social justice work involves. For example, social justice involves upholding fair treatment of people by addressing the issues that cause discrimination and inequality.[1] Additionally, the Australian social workers' *Code of ethics* recognises the importance of protecting the natural environment as part of peoples' wellbeing.[1] However, the natural environment is not regarded as having its own right to exist as part of social justice. Further, the *Code* falls short of recognising nonhuman animals' and Nature's rights.[2]

I like Iris Young's definition of justice as being reflected in the inclusion of people in decisions which impact them.[3] Nancy Fraser delves further into the processes required by explaining that the impacted parties need to be regarded as equal moral participants in addressing the justice issue.[4] For me, this is also about the environment and other animals as equal moral participants, albeit via the representations of advocates. The ethico-legal principle of procedural justice — sometimes called natural justice — brings attention to the need for authority figures to act in nondiscriminatory and accountable ways to protect individuals' rights.[5]

Social justice struggles are often organised around addressing the abuse of a minority status groups' human rights. There a number of important international ethical standards for all nations to uphold peoples' human rights. These include international conventions such as the *Universal Declaration of Human Rights*, the *Convention on the Rights of Persons with Disabilities*, and the *Declaration on the Rights of*

Indigenous Peoples.[6, 7, 8] Each statement is shaped by western ideas of individual human rights being upheld as integral to justice being experienced. However, peoples' rights are not assured. As just one example, there is increasing evidence of ecological conflict where human rights conflict with industry rights to access lands for mining. In these instances, humans, and other animals, communities, and the environment, tend to lose out.[9] There is no convention for the environment. This absence reflects the tendency to separate human rights and environmental rights. The United Nations' *Sustainable Development Goals* (SDG) have some value as an international statement of how to address the interlinked wicked problems facing the planet.[10] Thus, there is a need for sustainable cities and communities (SDG 11) which interlinks with the need for responsible consumption and production (SDG 12) so that climate change (SDG 3) is addressed. This, in turn, will positively influence decent work and the nature of economic growth (SDG 8), which may address gender inequality (SDG 5) and poverty (SDG 1).[10] As these socio-environmental issues are addressed, it is more likely that the Kyoto protocol will be upheld.[11] The protocol holds participating countries accountable to reduce their use of greenhouse gas emissions which cause climate change.[11] There is little evidence that Australia will meet the reduction commitments due mainly to our heavy reliance on the fossil fuels mining industry.

Australia is one of the most unequal nations in the world. As such, the costs of living in a capitalist society, which is reliant on unsustainable primary industries, is being borne by minority status groups. For example, poverty has increased in Australia and mainly impacts women and children financially dependent on Federal Government allowances which are below the poverty line. This equates to one in every eight people living in poverty.[12] Poverty is not on the national agenda as a matter requiring a substantial justice response. Although, there is some reporting in the media about the rising cost of living as interest rates continue to rise.[13]

Justice for other animals

Species justice is closely related to animal rights. Currently, there are no international conventions protecting animals' rights and wellbeing. As I've mentioned previously, the main barrier to justice for other animals is speciesism. The barrier of speciesism involves discrimination by people against other animals. Discrimination occurs due to the human species' superiority and power to control, use, and kill some species of animals for human consumption. The use of other animals is made socially acceptable through the belief that they are not equal, and therefore do not need to be afforded rights and feelings. Eaglehawk argues that there is no logic or moral basis that can justify the killing and consumption of other animals.[14] However, rational and moral arguments are not sufficient to change discrimination against some animal species. The power of socially sanctioned violence and the profit motivation of large scale animal farming overwhelms the moral power of arguments for animal rights.

Species justice, especially for animals with a commercial value, equates to a loving recognition of the equal intrinsic worth of all species, and thereby equates with no violence. I have suggested that veganism is one way to practice nonviolence towards other animals. It involves the refusal to use other animals for food, entertainment, research, clothing, and sport.[15] Additionally, a commitment to veganism involves working to dismantle the animal industrial complex of businesses, institutions, and governments who promote – or at least protect – the use of other animals. Alger suggests that veganism is a way to promote animal liberation alongside human liberation to the benefit of public health and environmental sustainability.[16] How this might be possible is the subject of her book. One previously mentioned example is the over-representation of migrant workers in abattoirs.[17]

Alger warns the practice of veganism has become implicated in its own politics.[16] Some vegans build a celebrity status which relies on financial contributions from other vegans, which often takes the focus away from the harm being done to other animals. It is one of the reasons why Alger argues that the vegan activist identity must die.[16] I do appreciate why she challenges vegans in terms of their role in the animal rights movement. At the same time, she acknowledges that many people who stand up to be counted for other animals' rights are not vegan. Upon reflection, what Alger is saying is that today I can't save a single animal on their way to an abattoir. Nor can I save one tomorrow or the next day. There is no immediate direct action I can take to make a difference to the millions of other animals who die each day across the planet for human consumption. Except not eating other animals. Simultaneously, I can support those who advocate for other animals' rights. Singer's new book *Animal liberation now* continues to uphold his earlier influential ideas that other animals feel pain; therefore, consideration of their interests should be afforded to them.[18] He now argues that global warming is such a threat that it makes more sense to encourage people to eat less meat.[18] Singer believes this would be more effective and immediate, in reducing greenhouse emissions due to methane from farmed cows, than trying to dismantle the animal industrial complex or trying to get people to practice veganism.[18]

It is morally wrong to allow the continuation of the mass scale slaughter of other animals. It is evidence of lovelessness and violence by the dominant species toward other species. hooks explains that change requires a conversion from an ethic of domination to an ethic of love.[19] There is a pressing need to develop a multispecies ethic that imagines a different way for societies and individuals to respond. One interesting writer in this space is Cynthia Willett who identifies four types of ethics to expand humans' ways of being with other animals.[20] She describes the idea of subjectless sociality where we suspend our individual sense of self to merge our awareness with other animals. When we do this we share a similar space or experience, as occurs during a flood or bushfire disaster.[20] The second ethic is intersubjective attunement, which refers to adjusting our behaviour to be in-step with other animals, to meet their needs and to gain their cooperation.[20] But not to gain their cooperation in order to hurt them. The third type of multispecies ethic requires us to cultivate a sense of beingness that does not overidentify with either the human body or the other animal's body.[20] For example, when other animals come to the aid of humans in trouble or when humans and other animals enjoy each other's company. In these instances, the bodily differences are second to the emotional exchanges. Finally, Willett explains we need to be willing to recognise, and make room for, the implications of animals as spiritual beings and as having agency to contribute to the world.[20] We know our pets have feelings, and research has shown this to be true for so many other animals.[21] In a nutshell, practising empathy for other species and regarding them as holding equal moral worth are two ways to challenge speciesism. Empathy and equal moral worth are part of what is needed to want to act and to avoid being complicit in the industrialised mass violence against some other animals. Many of us have pets whom we love and would do anything to care for them. Affording other animals this same love on a mass scale offers hope that change towards species justice is possible.

Justice for Nature

Justice for Nature, or environmental justice, can be best understood in terms of the presence of sustainability of communities, ecosystems, whole nations, and the planet. Capitalism, as an economic system, functions on economic unsustainability. This manifests as inequality between the workers and owners of the means of production. It also functions best with surplus labour that can be drawn upon as needed. The unneeded surplus labour join the unemployment statistics and are blamed for their lack of work. Social unsustainability, in part, takes the form of inequality in relation to how income is earned and how profits are made. It is also connected to prejudice, stigma, and violence in human relationships, as well as authoritarianism in human service organisations. The harm involved undermines the love and care needed to sustain relationships. Interrelatedly, environmental unsustainability is caused by inequality between Nature and the owners of primary industry businesses who gain their wealth from farmed animals and landscapes rich in minerals and ores. Nature is a finite resource. The mining of natural resources is not renewable or sustainable. The economic base directly influences citizens' socio-economic status and how they are valued. The capitalist economic base of society relies upon the exploited status of other animals and Nature. Thus, sustainability is not an abiding reality in capitalist societies.

The three types of sustainability are mutually reinforcing and need to be upheld for equality to be experienced. Social sustainability is equality between people and between people and other animals. Economic sustainability presents as nonviolence and nonexploitation by business owners, governments, and wealthy citizens towards other people and animals. Environmental sustainability manifests as mutual respect, love, and justice between people, other animals, and the natural world. The key point is that environmental justice requires these intersecting forms of sustainability. In turn, sustainability issues, as evident in wicked problems and all types of violence, need to be addressed for justice to be realised. It follows that social justice cannot be achieved without environmental and species justice. I agree with Rob White, who argues that it is a state crime if governments do not act to protect the environment from exploitation by private interests.[22] Many would not agree with this statement. But many people do agree. The environment movement provides a vital resistance to the unfettered pursuit of extreme wealth for the few. In Australia, most states have environmental protection legislation which contain an environmental precautionary principle. The principle enables governments to not proceed with approvals when to do so might cause irreparable harm or loss to the environment. A recent example is the restrictions required for the development approval of wind turbines in northern Tasmania to protect the migrating Orange Bellied Parrot.[23]

In societies where there is widespread social sustainability (i.e., social equality) between people, this is expressed through relationships characterised by love, nonviolence, and justice. The fostering of all types of sustainability is at the heart of First Nation Peoples' idea of stewardship. Poelina writes that Country is a living being who is an active participant in making the world through a complex and vast network of relationships.[24] These relationships need to be maintained, cared for, and protected from exploitation. Nature has agency.[24] Humans' relationship with Nature needs to be reviewed and re-shaped. First Nation Peoples' wisdom is premised on sustainability principles and love-informed ethics and relationships. This is a different economic system based on a respectful, nonexploitative relationship with Nature. Nature's ability to sustain life is under severe threat. Greta Thunberg's challenges to world leaders to do something epitomises the upcoming generations' concern for planetary survival. Social and economic wellbeing and fairness for humans, nonexploitation of other species, and protection of the environment are mutually reinforcing experiences. There is no justice without sustainability. Sustainability cannot be forced or gained by violence. Nonviolence and love are needed for sustainability to be achieved.

Expanding justice to include animals and the environment

The adoption of a more expansive idea of social justice is needed to include justice for other animals and the environment. This is not an idle academic exercise. Rather, it is a critical task to develop the ecological imagination and responses required to address the wicked problems of our time. Thomashow explains that an ecological imagination allows us to imagine new ways of being, to understand the interconnections between all elements of life, and engage with others to co-create new possibilities.[25] Wicked problems are composed of interconnected issues including poverty and famine, climate change, mining industry pollution, loss of biodiversity, and deforestation. The problems are wicked because there is no one solution. The seeming intractability of the problems makes them almost impossible to comprehend. However, this does not lessen the adverse impacts of these wicked problems. Holly Higgins coins the term ecocide, which includes 'eco' from oikos, meaning dwelling place in Greek, and the French 'cide' meaning killer.[26] She argues that we need to forcibly remove the systems and businesses that cause ecocide from exploiting and polluting the environment.[26] By forcibly removing systems and businesses, Higgins means using national and international legal interventions. Higgins' view is that human wellbeing is inter-related to ecological wellbeing. This is consistent with First Nation ideas where the natural environment, people, and other animals are intrinsically interwoven.[24] Poelina describes how, in her language, she belongs to the Mardoowarra River. She feels duty bound to protect the river because of the river's right to life. Poelina sees the river as a living being and as the river of life.[27]

Examples of justice for the environment are few and far between. A glimmer of hope for resistance working was provided by a group of young environmental activists, Youth Verdict.[28] They gained a major win in the Queensland Land Court with assistance from the Environmental Defender's Office. Recently, the Court ruled that the enormous Clive Palmer Waratah mine proposal in the Galilee Basin in western Queensland could not go ahead. The grounds for the decision included the cultural rights of the First Nations People and the human rights of future generations of young people to a sustainable environment.[29] It was a landmark ruling where, for the first time, Queensland's *Human Rights Act* 2019 had been used successfully. Youth Verdict argued for the protection of young peoples' rights due to the impacts mining and burning coal has on climate change. I was an interested bystander, along with hundreds of thousands of other Queenslanders, who were cheering everyone who enabled this justice outcome despite the odds.

Victories for the environment are not assured. They can be hard won and involve, in some instances, decades of activism with few tangible outcomes to show for the dedication. Sometimes, activists are required to make sacrifices in order to be heard or taken seriously. For example, Dawn Jecks is a private citizen who volunteered and led community-based mass nonviolent actions for more than ten years to protect fairy penguins from private development in Western Australia. Dawn lives near a coastal park, the Rockingham Lakes Regional Park, where fairy penguins live. The park was threatened by plans to develop the sensitive wetlands for a private mariner. It had government backing. The activist campaign slogan was 'Hands off Point Peron' and they eventually won, giving the park protection to this day.[30] Jecks spoke to me of her personal challenges over this decade-long struggle, where she placed her life on hold for the cause she felt compelled to do something about.

It is a truth that the ecosystems currently protected from exploitation and degradation are protected because of the activism of concerned citizens.

Eco justice practices

Love practices based on nonviolence principles interlink with a multispecies ethic to enable justice for all kinds. A range of skills and processes need to be utilised in justice work. Skills such as conflict resolution, problem-solving, negotiating, mediating, advocating, alliance building, and lobbying. These skills are integral to grassroots campaigns which are synonymous with community development work and social movements. The eco justice practices are indicative of the multi-pronged tactics and strategies needed to influence and change the elites who are benefiting from the injustice. Eco-activism is an umbrella term for concerned citizens joining together over a shared justice issue to bring about change by nonviolent methods.[31] Eco-activists hold a view that social, species, and environmental justice issues are interconnected and need to be addressed simultaneously. The justice goals need to be mirrored by the methods employed. The people impacted by the injustice need to be listened to and enabled to have a voice in the solutions being sought. A key capacity involves facilitating dialogue between the impacted minority group and the powerful stakeholders causing the justice issue. This dialogue needs to be undertaken between the interest groups as equals, but also with each group having different orders of responsibility to address matters of concern to the minority group. Where the justice issue centres on other animals and the environment, their interests need to be represented by allies from relevant justice organisations.

Justice will be done when it is seen to be achieved by the most impacted individuals and groups. It is not for the elites to say what is just or that it has been sufficiently realised. There can be an imperfect or partial justice in some circumstances. For example, in terms of environmental justice, when the environment has been severely polluted by radioactive substances that remain dangerous for thousands of years, there cannot be a perfect justice for Nature. There still is, however, a moral imperative to do what can be done to remediate the area and to cease using these substances. Some harms cannot be undone. But the harms must be avoided going forward, lessons learnt, responsibilities taken, apologies and reparations given. In terms of social justice, some First Nation People in Australia are calling for a truth commission as part of reconciliation with the white settlers. The belief is that until the nation faces the largely untold history of the colonial invasion, there can be no peace and healing. The call for truth-telling is an integral part of the current efforts to establish a treaty between the First Nation People of Victoria and the Victorian State Government.[32] There is no justice yet for Australia's First Nation People. Modern Australia has been built on unceded land. In terms of species justice for other animals, a partial justice has been achieved with the Federal Government, through stopping the live sheep export trade. However, the immediate consequences for existing herds of sheep as farmers destock is unknown and likely to be desperately distressing. For other farm animals, there is no immediate end to the live export industry. The industry is known to be about the cruel and unfair treatment of defenceless animals. Animal activists are continuing to lobby, research the adverse impacts, educate the public, and persist in their efforts to stop all live animal exports. The rights of other farmed animals to live free of exploitation are on activists' agendas. However, the elites of the industrial animal complex are fighting hard to maintain their businesses and profits.[33] There is no justice for farmed animals and many wild animals.

Eco justice can be realised in a range of ways by fostering a commitment to love and nonviolence. Eco justice links social, species, and environmental justice in recognition of the need to address the interconnectedness of human violence, species oppression, and environmental exploitation. Thus, for a love theory to guide responses to all forms of harm, we can't hold to a human-centric stance on who matters. Nevertheless, justice work that addresses social issues, matters. Failure to address violence caused by inequality between people makes justice for other animals and Nature seem more remote than ever. But because of the interconnectedness of people, places, and animals, justice work that succeeds for any group matters. It matters not only for the recipients of the justice outcomes, but for other minority status groups. Justice being upheld strengthens the moral fibre of a society and increases a shared faith in love power. This is because justice is not typically bestowed, rather, it has to be struggled for. The justice struggle is more likely to be successful when it is based on love and nonviolence. The means and methods of seeking justice by activists need to model the justice sought. This requires high order moral courage, persistence, and mass public support. Simultaneously, in our homes and all our relationships, we need to be fair and nonviolent.

A love-informed way of thinking about justice requires an ethical positioning that upholds the equal intrinsic worth of all beings and entities that comprise Nature and the totality of life on the planet. A multispecies ethic would regard the life of a tree as being as equally important as a human life and as equally important as another animal's life. To make this statement is one thing, to deeply believe in it is another, and to act on this belief is very difficult. Australia has a long way to go in equally valuing all sentient beings. Recently, culling has begun of Australia's wild brumby horses in the alpine areas of Victoria. The protests are muted in the general population but resistance by the Australian Brumby Alliance went to the highest court in the country.[34] They did not win. In this instance, the landscape was prioritised over the horses' right to live wild and free. Even so, it must be asked, did the horses need to be killed to resolve the issue? In this example, and all other justice struggles, love for the oppressed fuels challenges and resistances. Harmful, discriminatory laws, policies, and practices need to be challenged and resisted. Collectively, the nonviolent methods of justice work adds to the wisdom of what is needed for change towards love to be realised.

The equal intrinsic worth of all beings is not a position that is self-evident in western societies premised on the superiority of humans. Inter-relatedly, multispecies equal worth is not widely accepted in colonialist, patriarchal societies based on the superiority of white men and wealthy property owners. Further, in capitalist societies it is not self-evident or agreed that Nature and other animals have a right to exist without being considered only in terms of their use value to humans. This equal intrinsic worth premise places moral pressure on humans to regard and treat other animals as having rights to live peacefully and have their needs met. It also challenges us to regard and treat material entities, and other sentient beings, as having rights to co-exist without being exploited or harmed. These are by no means well-accepted moral positions.

I hold on to Simard's claim that trees are people as understood for millennia by the Subiyay people of Canada.[35] She sometimes refers to trees as tree people or the standing people. This way of thinking helps me maintain a resistive, ethical positioning against the tyrannies of eco injustices. Love which embraces the intersectionality of life on the planet is needed for justice to matter. Without this expansive commitment to love others and other places, untold tyrannies and unchecked exploitation would be rife. Tyrannies and exploitation are occurring right now, but would be far worse without millions of loving people working to enable justice, peace, and the survival needs and other rights of people, other animals, and landscapes.

A Theory of Revolutionary Love

FOR THIS BOOK, I tasked myself with developing a theory of love to address the issue of broken-heartedness. I understand broken-heartedness as a way of describing the harmful impacts arising from the interconnectedness of lovelessness, violence, and injustice. It may derive from one dimension of these three sources of harm, trauma, and loss. It may also derive from a mix of all three types of moral wrongs. I wanted a theory that was liveable and able to guide actions in all the situations where lovelessness might be found. Lovelessness, according to the theory, is the base level moral wrong from which other moral wrongs become possible. Lovelessness refers to the experience of the absence of love. It can take many forms, including withholding love and denying others their dignity, rights, and wellbeing. Lovelessness is closely related to violence of all types. If you love someone, you do not abuse them. If you love other animals, you do not eat them. If you love Nature, you do not exploit her to the point where she can't recover. Violences arising from lovelessness, in turn, are closely related to all forms of injustice. Unfair treatment of people, other animals, and Nature shows as issues of discrimination, inequality, destruction, and trauma. For these reasons a theory

189

of love needs to be revolutionary. It is not enough to love the powerless, the silenced, the exploited – the heart-broken – where the causes of the broken heart are not addressed. The dedication to address the causes of lovelessness, violence and eco injustice is a potentially revolutionary commitment. When many people make the dedication and act with love, nonviolence and ecojustice, social and environmental movements form and demand change. When one individual dedicates to love practices, they too, are contributing to building a society-wide belief in the power of love.

The challenge of theory into practice

I am asking a lot from a theory of revolutionary love. In doing so, I am perhaps setting unrealistic expectations about what one theory can do. However, I think that developing my ideas 'in situ' as I've grappled with my life and work challenges has resulted in an adaptable theory grounded in lived experiences. There is not the usual problem of a gap between the theory and how I practice. The theory of revolutionary love, at its current stage of development, is already working for me and the situations I find myself in. My individual actions are congruent with love practices in many different micro contexts. When I join with others these actions could scale up to the level of mass protest movements. The theory requires much more refining, but it has already stood the test of time. I put my confidence in how each of us is simultaneously grappling with how to make sense of our childhood experiences through to the wicked problems of society. Each of us are theory-builders and users of ideas that help us on our journey.

My ideas about love that I have shared with you are not widely accepted. But, I am far from alone. In fact, I have given many examples throughout the book of people I am inspired by and whose lead I am following. Putting love-informed ideas into practice can be very difficult, precisely because they are designed to challenge, resist, and change unjust situations. I am likely to meet backlash at every turn, especially where dominant interests are challenged – no doubt about it. It just means I will often resist and persist when change is slow or not possible. Further, what counts as loving action in any particular situation is not necessarily clear, and does not have a guarantee of success. While individual acts of love matter, justice work requires many like-hearted people as well as financial and other resources. This theory I have articulated needs to hold space for the other parties involved in the justice work to meet me on their own terms, with their own ideas and values. Thus, this is only half a theory. It is an open invitation to dialogue to share ideas, and to work together on shared concerns. Afterall, love is the willingness to learn, and to enable others' learning, for the highest good possible.

Summary of key ideas

Throughout the book, I've provided an ethical positioning that is congruent with hooks' idea of a love ethic. I've embraced and extended on her ideas to enfold nonviolence and ecojustice as necessary equivalent ethics. My personal and professional experiences and commentary on some of the pressing issues of our time have been offered to show the utility of these ethics. The utility rests in enabling my thinking about the issues and concerns and guiding how I acted or what I learnt. I want to distil the ideas into a succinct statement of a theory of revolutionary love for easy reference by interested readers. Typically, presentations of a theory show the assumptions and beliefs, principles, knowledge claims, practice strategies and limitations. The chapters on love, nonviolence and ecojustice include an end section on practice strategies, so I don't represent them here. The limitations of a theory of revolutionary love span from its idealism or over-simplification of complex, contested realities, to how hard it is to put into practice. I think there is some truth in these limitations. However, I think the theory will stand or fall on its own merits in real life situations. It is no reason to not offer theory when a knowledge gap exists in explaining broken-heartedness and showing ways to address its many manifestations.

I hope the summary below is sufficiently detailed for the dimensions of the theory to be clear and of value. While presented as a list that has a flow of logic to it, the dimensions can be read in any order. The image of a hologram where all the dimensions are interconnected and mutually informing would best suit how to think about the interrelationships.

> Love practices support life, wellbeing,
>   flourishing, equality, sustainability, and
>   peaceful co-existence.
> Love is needed for justice to matter.
> Justice matters because people, other animals,
>   and Nature are our Kin.
> As Kin, people, other animals, and Nature are of
>   equal moral worth. Therefore, it is morally

unacceptable if they are harmed and treated unfairly.

Harm, trauma and loss from injustice are indicators of violence.

Violence spans from the interpersonal level through to organisational and systemic violence, species exploitation, and environmental degradation.

Violence is morally indefensible.

Violence causes lovelessness, which involves devaluing the equal moral worth of others.

Lovelessness based on experiences of violence and injustice can be understood as broken-heartedness.

Powerful groups, organisations, and the elites of society gain from the inequality that underpins justice issues.

Gaining from inequality and privileges that accrue from inequality is morally indefensible.

The elites have a higher order of responsibility to address issues of injustice and harm.

Minority status groups have a lesser order of responsibility to raise the issues impacting them or to seek dialogue with the relevant parties.

Justice issues need to be raised and responded to in loving and nonviolent ways to avoid repeating patterns of harm.

A theory of love is needed because of the complex, intersecting nature of the harm caused by violence and injustice. No one idea or value will be enough to ensure a critical understanding of the power issues.

A theory of love is premised on three interrelated and mutually reinforcing cherished ideas: Love. Nonviolence. Eco Justice.

Ideas become guideposts to moral actions, and hence ethics, when put into practice: Ethic of love. Ethic of nonviolence. Ethic of eco justice.

It is about love for three kinds of beings: People. Other animals. Nature. Where Nature is inclusive of people and other animals.

This entails a commitment to address: Lovelessness. Violence. Eco Injustice.

By individuals, groups, communities, organisations, businesses, and societies by practising:

Self-love. Love of others, including other animals and Nature. Nonviolence and resistance. Justice work. Creating safe workplaces and fostering trauma-informed care. Multispecies ethics. Sustainability and protection of biodiversity.

All forms of justice work involve some mix of challenging with love, resisting with love, and changing with love.

These practices are likely to be unwelcome if
  perceived to not be in the interests of the
  elites of society.
Therefore, anticipating backlash and knowing
  how to minimise it when experienced from
  the powerful and privileged groups is crucial
  in justice work.

What makes love revolutionary?

Love is the life force of the planet. Love is a creative, relational
and co-constituting type of power that is expressed by
agential beings of all kinds. Actions that are loving, nonviolent,
and justice-seeking are potentially revolutionary. For the
revolutionary potential to be realised, there needs to be a
substantive increase in experiences of love, safety, justice, and
wellbeing by oppressed minority groups, other animals, and
Nature. Beings who experience broken-heartedness know the
importance of love. They know the pain and harm due to the
absence of love. When the broken-hearted pivot on pain and
harm and express love out into the world, it is revolutionary.
It is a higher order of ethical wisdom to transform their
broken-heartedness into love energy instead of hate energy.
Violence breeds violence. But violence that has caused harm,
when defied and harnessed for love of others, turns harmful
power into loving power. In this way, nonviolence matches and
neutralises violence. The responsibility for addressing violence
rests with humans. Yet humans are not the only beings able to
act to re-balance from harm and destruction. Nature is the best
example we have of revolutionary love because she is the totality

of the creative life force of the planet. Nature encompasses all intelligences and all diversity of ways of being.

The unsung human leaders of the love revolution are beings who experience broken-heartedness and pivot on that deep pain and loss towards love. But just how does this happen? It surely seems to be an extremely difficult thing to do.

Pivoting to love from broken-heartedness

Broken-heartedness has many causes and may be understood by people in different ways. As an idea that explains painful experiences, it has to have value for us in our personal lives as well as in our work lives. We all negotiate loss at some level while trying to accept the profundity of life and dying and death.

When my sister died from cancer, it was a very very sad time. For her, the sadness had no bounds in her battle to survive. She struggled through the pain and loss of her strength and dreams, knowing she would be leaving her family behind. It is still hard to find words for how I feel almost two years later. I have no words for how it must feel for her adult sons and their families, and for my mum and one of my other sisters. It does not seem fair that such a beautiful person should die so young. We all miss her deeply. This is a type of heartbreak many of us know and live with as best we can.

Then another deeply sad thing happened. My brother, just a year younger than my sister, died suddenly. His heart had broken when our sister died. He was having difficulty moving forward in life without her. Just weeks before, he had taken her ashes home to her place out in western Queensland. All he needed to do to help lay her to rest was done. Then he was gone. Just three months after her. The searing pain, on top of the, still raw, loss of our sister, was shattering. For his partner and adult children, and for our mother. For my sister's sons who were leaning on him after their mum died. He had a grand Christmas day with family. Just as he loved to do. Then later the next day, when trying to repair a broken down work ute, it fell on him. He died instantly. No chance to help him. No chance to say goodbye. No chance to tell him how grateful and impressed we all were with how he cared for our sister. All I can say with certainty is that both my sister and brother knew they were loved.

There is also the heartache of lost loves and relationships that do not last where there were shared high hopes and dreams. A relationship in my family broke down. Thankfully, no children were involved, but the break did leave behind one devastated person. He did not see it coming. She took a long time to acknowledge to herself it was not working and was distraught to see his devastation. His heart simply shattered. He died, but was somehow still breathing. Our family member did not want to keep breathing. There seemed no point. There was nothing to live for without the one person he truly loved. Both his stepfather and a friend of his had died by suicide when their respective relationships broke up. Where was a male who had survived such a big loss, who could show him how to keep going, when his heart had broken? He was not able to work, he had nowhere to live, no money, and a car that was barely road-worthy. To walk away with nothing, somehow, it would be something worse than nothing. He would be walking away without her. It felt unfair to him. There was no domestic violence. There was love for the longest time. Now he is living without the love he had, but with something different gradually taking shape. He is living with immense courage and a still very broken heart. He is learning to love himself slowly, very slowly. He is one of the most impressive people I know. So is his now ex-partner. She has stepped into unknown territory of the heart by loving herself when it meant she needed to let go of a dear, good person in her life. Slowly, very slowly, she is finding her way in the world as her authentic self.

None of us have to look very far to see other people who know heartache. Looking inwards, we can all recognise losses, and sometimes extreme distress, in our own hearts. Sometimes, this distress is what we have done to others, including people we love. Many of us have found ways to live with our heartache, but not everyone finds a way. We can't always be there for someone else. We do not always show up for ourselves. There are so many permutations of the nature of heartache and how we respond to it. I am particularly concerned with experiences of heartache caused by violence and injustice where the heartache compounds into broken-heartedness. Broken-heartedness of this type involves the pain of knowing lovelessness. The loss of loved ones is anchored in the same place in our hearts where the loss related to violence and injustice resides.

How do we, then, keep going with so much pain and sorrow in our hearts? How do I keep going with the pain of my personal and professional losses? I think I have done it, and am doing it, by pivoting. It is a bit of an unusual word, pivoting. It may conjure images of a ballet dancer turning on their toes without moving off the spot. In ballet, this turning of the whole body without moving a foot or both feet is called a pirouette. There are lots of ways of pivoting. The main point is the idea of turning in a new direction using a countering energy. A complete about-face, so to speak. And so, on the pain of a sudden and deep loss, we use that same pain to be gentle with ourselves, or we use it to be sensitive to others who have experienced that loss too. The pain may be so unbearable you just want to scream and shout out loud. This is understandable. It is not what I mean by pivoting. That is directly expressing the pain – again, understandable. However, if you are screaming and shouting at another person or an animal, that is not okay. That is spreading the pain. To pivot on the energy of wanting to scream and shout, it might look like turning on your favourite music, turning the volume up loud and screaming and shouting until your throat is red raw. You have shifted your energy, your pain, and dissolved it, at least for now. This is not about denying or minimising the pain. Rather, it is about drawing on the pain energy and making it into something else. There are too many examples of people acting on their pain by spreading it out into the world and causing untold misery, loss, and fear. This reality puts a sombre note on what I am saying, and reminds me that to pivot on pain is not an easy or certain way to keep going with a broken heart.

I want to acknowledge a type of pivoting from broken-heartedness that is loving and paying it forward to others. This is where we transform our heartache and pain by pivoting on the pain energy and being loving, both to ourselves and to someone else. It can be extremely difficult to transform your pain into love and then pay it forward. Pivoting on our pain and releasing it in a nonharmful way is inspiring to me. Just this week, I was chairing an examination for a higher degree candidate's research proposal. Her research topic was on choirs and their therapeutic value to the singers. Part of the presentation included an impromptu video of choir members leaving the space after a singing session. Each person was invited to say how they were feeling. It was inspiring and beautiful. Person after person was shining and happy and expressed joy, upliftment, peace, connection – so many different but similar feelings. The singers were all ages, genders, ethnicities, and with health and other life challenges. The joy and upliftment transformed their pain, and many said it was the highlight of their week. The singers were pivoting on their own personal life challenges by singing in the choir. I have had the privilege of listening to hundreds of peoples' stories during my lifetime. Each and every person has a story to tell, and each and every person was grappling with heartache. People can keep living with the heartache of enormous pain and loss. They can be trying to be good people, trying to get help, or trying to understand something. So many inspiring people practising how to be loving.

One of the most challenging pivoting experiences for me in my personal life related to my family member. When they lost the will to live, it was very confronting, frightening, and devastating to witness. I was right in the middle, literally, of his relationship break-up with his partner. He was like a son to me. She was my daughter. In my professional life, I can usually be sure of a safe, quiet place when I come home at the end of the day. Time to catch my breath, to reflect on anything that might still be troubling me, and to recharge ready for the next work day. But that safe, quiet place disappeared. My own family and household turned upside down, and the two people I loved most in the world were in such turmoil. It was the worst of times. I knew from all my years as a social worker that I could not save anybody, that it was not my responsibility. But nor could I stand by and do nothing. To witness the minute-by-minute struggle of my family member to survive was extremely impactful. His pain radiated off him. I could hardly breathe when sitting with him as he expressed his deep wounding. The situation had ripple effects for all of us over many months.

What I want to share with you about this is how my family member taught me something precious. He taught me, without even trying to, that love matters. I, of course, knew this, but I had not been so deeply tested on my belief in love until that time. Little by little, he showed me that love is enough. Even when that love is not from who you wanted it to be from. It was from her mother. For me, it was somewhat strange to be suddenly so central in his world. His world had collapsed and changed in a way that was barely recognisable. I knew it was not my love that he wanted. But it was my love that he got. And he accepted it. I was definitely broken-hearted for him, and for my daughter. But also for myself. I remember very clearly how I used pivoting. I was consciously noticing the pain in my heart, and choosing kindness, patience, hope, forbearance ... love. I showed him these things even when I had almost no energy left to believe in these life-affirming ideas. I held on tight to the ideas, especially hope, until he could find the heart to hold them for himself. As I said, he is truly an impressive person.

The need for loving places and professionals

Recently I read in the local newspaper that a young woman – Courtney Morison – died at just 22 years of age. Courtney had died by suicide.[1] She had been trying to get help from the Townsville mental health unit. Her sister explained that Courtney had been struggling with her mental health for years but knew when she needed to reach out for help.[1] Courtney's mother and sister expressed their outrage about the system letting Courtney down by dismissing the seriousness of the situation as behavioural. It is also behavioural when someone dies by suicide.

The Queensland State Government's Health Minister is reported as saying there is much the government needs to do to improve the state's mental health services. The systems and resources issues are known. A full clinical, internal review was promised but it will find what is already known. Chances are nothing will change. This is not about finger pointing. It is not about who made the decision to discharge Courtney, even though she was pleading for help because she was self-harming. But a life has been lost. A mother's heart has been broken. Has a duty of care been offered to her? The public's confidence in the mental health system has, once again, been negatively impacted.

To address lovelessness, we need to make the place that is meant to care to actually be caring when a person's life is on the line. We need to make the place that is meant to be safe actually be safe and have enough beds, especially when a person is feeling unsafe and asking to stay in the hospital. It is such a maddening system when many people are forced to be in mental health facilities and do not want to be. While many other people want, or their carers want them, to be in hospital, and are not able to be admitted or not permitted to stay until their health and safety has stabilised. Systems can't be changed overnight. The professionals who interacted with Courtney made the judgement that it was a behavioural issue, and, therefore, not something they could help with. This is an indefensible decision and they do hold some responsibility. So too do their supervisors, service managers, policy and resource leaders, the Chief Psychiatrist, and the Minister for Health. So does society, and myself as part of this society. The specific and shared responsibilities were not upheld enough to help Courtney.

The collective consequence was a young person feeling as though the system lacked love for her – in Courtney's words, "they won't help me".[1] When you love somebody, you help them. If you can't help them, this does not absolve you of some responsibility if you do not try to ensure they have someone who can. Discharge from a mental health facility is a known high risk time for patients. Courtney was being supported by a case manager in the community. They would have loved her. Was this person involved in Courtney's discharge in some way so Courtney felt someone was looking out for her? Was someone looking out for Courtney's mother and sister during this very distressing time? The justice outcome can't only be a report that shows some service gap and a recommendation to address it. An expression of condolences by the Minister for Health is acknowledged, but is not enough love for the loss and injustices involved.

I am no-one to Courtney's family. I am only connected to them through a news report. Despite that, I do feel a connection. I have expressed this connection by including Courtney's death here in this book. First of all because she matters. Second, because it is too easy to not read what I knew was going to be a very sad and unjust media piece – on the front page of the newspaper, the headlines were shocking, "Woman dead within hours of discharge: Hospital death trap".[1] But I read it because

I knew it would be devastating, and that it would be worse if I tried to ignore it. I must not let myself become uncaring. Third, because it may help someone else – perhaps you, or someone you know and love.

I know this next statement to be true: it can just take one person who had direct contact with Courtney in hospital to make the difference. This is not to oversimplify the system complexities or the seriousness of what Courtney was struggling with. I knew a person, whom I will call Sam, who has a lived experience of mental illness. He told me some of his extremely sad but ultimately most transformative story. Sam did not say much, but enough for me to never forget what he said and to never forget him. Sam, who had been in and out of mental health facilities all his adult life, said that no-one took the time to help him. That is the extremely sad part. I can't even comprehend how he has managed to stay alive. He told me how he would cope with being hospitalised by sitting in a hunched over, mute-like trance. Not engaging with anyone, not responding to anything. Then came the pivoting influence in his life. Over a few weeks, a nurse came and sat down beside him whenever he was on a shift on the ward. The nurse did not try to make him talk. He did not try to tell Sam to do something. He just sat with him. Sometimes it was just a few minutes. Other times it was for many minutes, even half an hour. The nurse's presence seeped into the patient's awareness and heart. As the receiver of Sam's story, it seemed like he felt love from the nurse. Whatever name he would put to it, the crucial thing was, he was able to pivot from being hunched over, closed off, and defended. Sam said from that point on he began to reclaim his life. I met him some years later. He was helping me provide education to mental health clinicians. He had this role due to his lived experience of mental illness where his perspective of what help needs to look like was crucial for the clinicians to hear. Again, another impressive person. So too was the nurse whose loving professionalism helped Sam turn his life around.

Sam's story had a forever-after transformative impact on me. I had been educated in all sorts of knowledge and skills, and could listen to, and talk with, people in many distressing circumstances. But it was often clear to me that what I said was not enough or not going to change anything for the better. After hearing Sam's story, I recognised how important it is to be with other people in their distress. Not to rush to put words on what they could not name, because it was too big and too overwhelming for them to name. Not to think I had the answer for them. I forget sometimes and find myself speaking too much, not listening enough. Then I remember what Sam told me. I pivot back to being present for the person before me.

It is a never-ending kind of dedication, being loving. This includes learning what this means and what it needs to involve in every interaction with others and ourselves. As one person in the world, it can seem insignificant what I do and what I think. But I know it always matters. I may not have always done enough for, or the right thing by, someone, a place, and some animals. But here and now I have another chance: to act with love; to refuse to retaliate when someone hurts me; to be willing to extend myself to be there for someone, even when I am out of energy. I can also acknowledge and give my support to other people who are doing good in the world. Not everyone who is doing good – or what I call being a love revolutionary – has a public profile, they quietly get on with their lives. This is how it is for most of us.

Acknowledging those who have influenced me

As you may have noticed, a lot of my source of hope and learning has come from books. Many of the books and other references I have mentioned in this book have contained ideas that have significantly shaped my life. I have given some examples of impressive people who are authors and advocates, pivoting on their pain and acting not with anger borne of pain towards others, but with loving ideas and ways. I want to particularly acknowledge some of the authors as a way of summarising the key messages of the book. Izzeldin Abuelaish lost his children in a bomb attack by the Israelis on his house. He continued to be a dedicated doctor to both his own people in the Gaza Strip and to the Israeli people. He wrote that to retaliate would not bring his daughters back. He believed that hatred is a moral wrong and stands in the way of peace.[2] His book title says it all — *I shall not hate*. Rather, he pivoted towards love and service every day in his work. I hold Izzeldin's story close and keep the title of his book right at the front of my mind. Love is, first and foremost, about not causing harm. It is also about acting with critical understanding, compassion and nonviolence.

Behrouz Boochani is a Kurdish journalist who was seeking asylum in Australia but was deported to off-shore detention on Manus Island. During the six years he was detained, he experienced and witnessed extreme suffering and dehumanisation. Behrouz wrote a book which heavily criticised the Australian Government.[3] It won a national book award. The task of writing was particularly challenging – he had a hidden phone to type scraps of thoughts into, and, when he could, he would send these scraps to literary friends in Australia on WhatsApp. The dedication and desperation that imbued every word is palpable in his book. Behrouz is an incredible example of how a person with a broken-heart turned away from despair and trauma hundreds and hundreds of times to write on WhatsApp. His contribution to educating the Australian public, and me, on the tyrannies of off-shore detention is as significant as Michel Foucault's writing on prisons and mental hospitals. Love is about resistance against terrible harms and injustices. Love is about truth-telling. Love is about people not allowing their government to act in loveless ways towards people seeking asylum from persecution.

Anne Poelina is a First Nation person from the north west of Western Australia. She describes herself as belonging to the Mardoowarra River and as having a custodial duty to care for the river. Anne writes about how the river is a living being and part of a tapestry of natural beings who are considered relatives of First Nation People. She is a contemporary leader in Australia showing how we need to have empathy for all living beings and as part of this how we need to learn how to coexist with Nature "and not own, dominate or exploit her."[4] For this to be achieved non-Indigenous Australians need to understand how the human-made laws are not the first law, rather according to traditional ecological knowledge, the first law is the law of the land. An invitation is offered by Anne for non-Indigenous Australians to be willing to listen to Nature and to share in the custodial work with First Nation People. Love is responding to wise human and nonhuman beings' invitations to join the caring responsibilities for our planet.

Kristy Alger is an animal rights activist and author of a book I often comment on because of her insightful ideas about the animal industrial complex.[5] Kristy's activism places her in the direct line of the suffering of other animals, and, as a vegan, she is a shining light in the animal rights movement. She lives with the outrage of harm done to other animals, with her day to day life entwined with an awareness and, often active, witnessing of this profound loss and trauma. I can't do what Kristy does. I can't go to abattoirs and literally rescue animals from pens before they are slaughtered. Kristy's dedication reminds me I could do more to support people like her and her important activism borne of love for other animals. Love needs to be practised at home, at work, and with all our Kin.

Janet Meagher is one of scores of people with a lived experience of mental illness who provided a witness statement to the Victorian Royal Commission into the state's mental health services.[6] Janet pivoted from her trauma and pain from how she was treated during many hospitalisations. She used her anger to fuel her decades-long activism and won the Australian Mental Health Prize in 2018, which she shared with Professor Allan Fels. People with lived experience of mental illness who take up a public profile are some of the most courageous people I know. Janet's award with a person who has professional knowledge and expertise, sends a message about the equally important knowledge and expertise that comes from a person's own life experiences. Love is about turning experiences of torture in the guise of care into advocacy for minority groups' human rights. This type of love challenges violent discourses and structures.

Suzanne Simard is a botanist whose scientific research on how trees talk to each other was born of her concern about the destruction of forests. Even though her family survived by harvesting logs from Canada's forest, Simard pivoted from her heritage and the usual career trajectory of conventional forest management. She closely listened to the forest and studied its secrets to discover how trees communicate and connect with each other. Underground fungal networks carry biochemical messages between trees. Simard explains how the mother tree is the centre of communication in the forest who passes messages on to her Kin to warn them, to protect them, and to enable them to survive.[7] Simard's work deeply shifted my understanding about the sentience of nonhuman beings. It helped me know that my belief in the equal moral worth of all of Nature was based on a truth of epic proportions. Nature has agency and wisdom and gives life. Some of my best friends are tree people. Love is evident in how Nature creates and sustains life.

bell hooks wrote about growing up in a racially segregated America as a Black woman and her heart ache from lack of love as a child. She dedicated her life to writing to her people about the importance of self love and loving Blackness. Her ability to write in an accessible way when exposing the costs of white supremacy and patriarchy meant her influence was enormous. She was recognised as one of the most significant writers of the last 50 years when she died in late 2021. hooks' idea of the love ethic has substantially shaped my life and work. Where there is love there will be no oppression.[8] Love is the answer and the way, no matter the issue and no matter who it is an issue for.

No doubt about it, the ideas and books, and the amazing authors I've shared with you have been my friends at key points in my life. Right beside the books and their authors are the people I have met in my work. As a social worker, listening to people and their stories has been my way of staying connected to my people, my Kin. Story by story, meeting by meeting, I learned precious lessons on the power of love. When nothing else could be done, I could be with the person. I could listen. Listening is love in action. The answer in any situation will have a dose of love. But it has to be freely given and received – without coercion or hidden agendas — co-created in relationship and in the moment, and for it to be repeated over time and across all our multispecies relationships.

More to learn

Love is certainly a complex idea. It means different things to different people. Even as I've shared with you my thinking about love, I am aware there is so much more to learn and understand. The end of the book is not pronouncing that my learning has finished or that I have done justice to this topic. I continue to see broken-heartedness caused by lovelessness, violence, and injustice in the world. I also see people transforming deep pain and trauma by pivoting on that pain and trauma, and paying it forward as love. This to me is the heartbeat of revolutionary love. When hurt people refuse to hurt others, love themselves, and love the world around them, there is an enormous amount of harm being healed and love being gifted. It remains the case, though, that the elites of society have a different order of responsibility to address their privileges and abuses of power that cause inequality, harm, and destruction. Failing to do so leaves a gaping wound in the people, between species, and in all of Nature. It also leaves an unfair burden on the broken-hearted to call for redress to issues of violence and injustice. In the epilogue, the personal essays show how I try to take my proper responsibility for the personal and professional situations where I have experienced or caused broken-heartedness.

Epilogue: Personal Essays

From fortressed heart to being loved back

No-one has ever asked me about what it has been like being single for almost half my long life. I grew up believing I would get married, raise a family, and my partner and I would love each other deeply and remain together. This was not my story. That I have been a single person in a society that professes the values of coupledom and family, is an interesting part of who I am. But it is not interesting for the surface reality of what it means, but for what it hides. Like most young women growing up in western societies, I had a romanticised and sexualised idea of love. These ideas persisted against the odds of witnessing violence mixed with love between my parents and awkward first loves as a teenager. Later, in my early thirties, I am now embarrassed to recall, I travelled to another country, without an invitation, to visit with someone special. I had met them while they were travelling in Australia and fell in love with their adventurous spirit and beautiful photography of wild places in central Australia. I had convinced myself maybe they were the one. They ticked all the boxes. One problem, I was not entirely welcomed. I clearly did not fit their idea of a partner or even someone to hook up with again. I can still feel the deep anguish when this unwelcome reality seeped into my heart which shattered into a million pieces, coloured with shame for being so foolish. I left suddenly and without saying goodbye – on a Greyhound bus, of course. Never before in such a public place, and so far from home, had I cried so hard and for so long. This was not the first time I had gone out of my way and off my life plans to try to connect with a love interest. But this was definitely far out of my way – to the other side of the world. That is what I am embarrassed about, that I thought I could make something happen or that I had to go get the relationship, no matter the cost to me.

In what became a profoundly life-changing rebound, I met a person on my return from that far away place – backpacking with a small group of travellers from a youth hostel in the Grand Canyon (amazing place, by the way). They were loud, opinionated, dripping with gold jewellery that they had made. We had spare time and became good travel buddies. They were kind, thoughtful, and creative, so the fact they were coming down from prescription meds didn't quite register in my consciousness. We travelled back to Australia together. I married them so they could stay here. Looking back on it all, it is quite easy to see I wasn't thinking clearly. Fast forward three years and we had a child together. I had not expected to have children. I believed there were enough little people in my life to love due to my extended family. So, our daughter was a remarkable gift and turned my life into a more meaningful and loving one than I ever thought was possible.

The loss is that her parents' relationship did not hold. The reasons may well be seen differently by each of us. But I was

100% determined that there would be no violence in my home where I was raising a child. I called time on the relationship with my partner when there were warning signs. It was the hardest thing I have ever done. I wanted our daughter to grow up and know and love both her parents. But I was not going to let history repeat into another generation of domestic violence for both myself and her other parent. We created a loving and safe family across two households, but we did not seek thereafter to re-establish our personal relationship. We remained friends and friendly, until some years later when harsh judgements and threats against our daughter – from my perspective – resulted in me severing that commitment to maintain our friendship.

I have not re-partnered to create a family, blended or otherwise, since. I have not looked for, or been approached to be in, an intimate relationship with anyone. I puzzle about how this has come to be, and can only surmise I must have put up the most powerful fortress against such intimacy. Initially, due to my dedication to raising my daughter in a safe and loving home. This was an all-encompassing dedication as a predominantly single parent (not to take away from the enduring relationship our daughter has with her other parent). However, my heart remained fortressed long past it being needed to raise a loved and phenomenally beautiful young woman. The loss I am referring to is the loss of potential for our daughter to experience two dedicated people able to love each other without violence, and with justice imbuing all aspects of their relationship.

The other dimension to my broken-heartedness was my inability to form a safe and loving relationship with my partner. This loss still sits heavily in my heart, for the depth of loss spreads across the passing years. We will not grow old together.

We have not enjoyed sharing all the moments of our daughter growing up. If it was not to be a family with her other parent, then could it be with another loving person? It seems not.

I can't say I believe in love, if by love we are referring to a commitment with another adult in an intimate and personal relationship. Maybe my desire for such a relationship has died long ago – died in the ashes of a broken heart when my marriage failed. Nevertheless, I do know love in many forms and intensities. Maybe, because I am single, I have been afforded many opportunities and freedoms to meet, be with, sometimes help, and sometimes experience joy and peace with other people, other animals, and Nature. I think of my experience of knowing love as a mutual give-and-receive relationship that fortifies, validates, recognises, stands with, and connects with another being in a myriad of ways – no matter how fleeting, and especially if it endures over time. I would say I have not known loneliness, or pointlessness, or complete despair since my daughter came into my life. I was on the planet nearly forty years before she was born, and my heart was well and truly broken into tiny pieces by then. A large part of my heart healing is due to being her mother, friend, business partner, coffee buddy, and house mate.

There is a part of me that I may not be giving enough credence to in terms of my personal relationship with love. I have seen so much trauma, loss, and grief caused by how people treat each other, other animals, and Nature. I simultaneously understand yet cannot figure out why we, as a people, do not do more to change what we know to be wrong and harmful. As just one devastating example, Black deaths in custody in Australia continue at an appalling rate despite recommendations from the first inquiry decades ago. The solutions are known. The violence continues. I think I have turned away from the pure misery of such situations to protect myself, to try to keep my sanity. But each time I turn away and do nothing, my capacity for love diminishes. Maybe it is not possible to live and to have a fully open heart at all times in the face of deep loss and harm. I have certainly had incredible teachers in how to love from beings with broken hearts who keep on living the best lives they can. But, I have always met people and other beings on my own terms. Presumably, this is not a good starting point for an equal, loving relationship.

I have so defended my heart from more loss that I have lost some hope of ever resting in what Thich Nhat Hanh calls true love with other people. At the same time, the love I believe in most assuredly is the beauty, power, and life-giving force of Nature. She remains the underpinning and all-pervasive source of hope and wellbeing for me. When I wrote this last sentence, thinking I wanted to believe it, I doubted if I meant it. I did not want to have to say I feel totally unloved.

A few weeks have passed since I claimed that the love I believe most assuredly in emanates from Nature. During that time, I read a section in one of the most inspiring books on my bookshelf – Robin Wall Kimmerer's *Braiding sweetgrass*.[1] She writes about a workshop she was facilitating with environmental science students. They all showed much respect and care for Nature. But when Wall Kimmerer asked them if Nature loved them, the students were not sure what to say. Pressing them more on this, they came to realise that if this was so, then we must be sure to not harm her. Because you do not harm who loves you. She explains that when we recognise the two way relationship, it becomes a sacred bond.[1]

When I read that Nature loves us back, I was so surprised, but immediately knew it to be true. I felt great excitement and rushed to share it with my next class of students. Fortunately, it was a subject based on an ecological approach to social work that places other animals and Nature alongside people as having equal moral worth and concern. The students also rushed to share their similar sense of being loved by Nature, and this proved to be a pivot point of intimately learning that Nature is a living, loving being. I now know I was not grasping at Nature as my main hope of being loved. She really does love me, just as I love her. These words of Wall Kimmerer pierced through my heavily fortressed broken heart. The words instantaneously re-aligned and healed the brokenness, knowing that all my life I have been held in Nature's embrace. I experienced my heart opening greatly to the ever-present reality of her loving me. Her love is multi-dimensional, and includes the greatest gift of all, the gift of giving me and others life. Wall Kimmerer's book is full of her loving ways with Nature and, in return, Nature's loving ways with her. In their commendation Gilbert describes Wall Kimmerer's book as "a hymn of love to the world".[1] I too agree.

From expert helping to un-professionalising love

There is a seriously worrying disowned dimension to who I am. This relates to my professional identity as a social worker. I grew up in a big family, and did not intend to have children for a long time in my adult life. Instead, I dedicated myself to my career of helping others. A noble dedication, one might say. As a young adult, I was a perfect example of what some call the walking wounded. I did not fully appreciate the significance of this for many years. Meanwhile, I placed myself in incredibly powerful positions as a social worker. This made me privy to other peoples' woundedness – what I now call, broken-heartedness. Why is this a problem, you might ask. Aren't most people in the helping professions dealing with their own traumas and heartbreak as they try to help others? Wouldn't having similar experiences to clients make it easier to be empathic and supportive?

I do not like the term client. But I think I should use it here, as I am wanting to speak from a place of being in a professional role with people I meet in a client role. What is important in this essay is what I can own and take responsibility for about my way of being with other people in professional situations. I do want to acknowledge that in the interpersonal spaces social workers share with other people, much good can happen. But, much harm can happen as well. While not the sole province of social work, the idea of emotional imperialism encapsulates something of what I mean. Frayn explains emotional imperialism as a moral snobbery where professionals presume to know what others need, or what they should think and do.[2]

It may seem like a dramatic overstatement to make, but imperialism, in its various forms, and the supporting oppressive systems, hold all types of violence in place. Systemic racism is held in place by cultural imperialism of the dominant, settler, racial group. Members of the dominant group repress and deny the humanity, ideas, and sovereignty of the colonised traditional owners of a country. The presumption to know better, to be able to help, to be the expert, can hide many tyrannies. Perhaps there is none worse than the power and privilege of what a professional, helping qualification gives. The professional privilege gives the needed authority to control, refuse services, incarcerate, diagnose, medicate, remove children from families, and so on.

Social work is a career that requires much in terms of the practitioner, and rightly so. As a profession, social work has had its own share of being criticised. Richan and Mendelsohn capture some of the dimensions of critiques that ring ever-truer over the decades. They describe social work as the increasingly unloved profession, not only by clients, but also by peers and even itself.[2]

What can I say in social work's defence? Do I want to defend my own profession? Currently in my academic role, I am trying to pivot off these kinds of critiques to centre the practice of love in the social work curriculum. This is not a widely supported content focus, but it seems particularly strange to me that, of all professions, social work has not laid claim to being a loving profession. There are many reasons for this, and I personally believe love has always mattered in many social workers' motivations and actions, even if not given this name. But in social work's rush to professionalise, to build an empirical knowledge base, and be registered as a recognised discipline in the human services sector, emotionally broad and thrown-about words such as love have no place.

I also know that much of the problem for the client is beyond their control due to the impact of inequality and discrimination. Nevertheless, they are often expected to be responsible for the problem at the same time. It took a long time for me to recognise how implicated I am in this positioning of the client as the problem. Correct, I was not totally naive about this pattern of problematising clients or victim-blaming. I held on to the idea by Nicholas Ragg that social work is about "people, not cases".[3] In my mind and actions, I was always trying to connect in an authentic and relevant way. Is being authentic enough though, when the costs of being a client can be so high? As I have mentioned, in western capitalist countries like Australia, there is a stigma related to seeking help. While the intensity of the stigma can vary, seeking help related to emotional and mental health issues is highly stigmatised. What this can mean is that people in the client role who engage with, for example, the mental health system, can feel dehumanised. They can lose their dignity, or experience a loss of face and autonomy. Such that, even if I am aware of this and treat people with great respect and care, the stigma is still pervading our relationship. It is true that some professions experience a kind of parallel stigma against the practitioners. But it is not the same – I am getting paid, and am expected to manage the emotional costs of my employment.

I, myself, do everything I can to avoid being in a client role. In fact, I have not very often approached someone for professional help. I have nearly always engaged with people in client roles where I have professional authority over them. Yes,

I tried to make sure the person felt heard and supported to be self-determining, and always according to what I deemed appropriate. There were costs to them that did not also accrue to me. In fact, I always benefited from clients, not the least because I got paid for seeing them.

This might seem harsh and simplistic, but I know I am not being unfair to myself here. The disowned part of me in my professional role is not so much what I did or did not do. The disowned part is the client in me. This is who I am writing to. There are two dimensions to disowning my client self. The first dimension is the denying of other people, other beings, the opportunity to help me. I have done it seriously tough on many occasions, when putting out my hand to ask for help would have made such a difference. I find the second dimension much more troubling. Since the earliest days in my career, I was aware of how much I gained from interactions with people in the client role. This might seem an absurd thing to say. Some of the clients I engaged with have been so distressed, or hopeless, or helpless, or aggressive – how could I have gained anything from them?

To be present for them, I have had to learn how to be detached from my own issues. This is most proper. What happened over many years was truly unexpected. In my professional work, I heard about other peoples' fears, family, and life challenges in all their diversity and uniqueness. To say clients helped me gain a perspective is too trite, and understates what their collective gift was for me. Rather, I could place myself with others, albeit in a very specific set of circumstances that curtailed the sharing that was possible. I found my human Kin, so to speak. I did not feel lonely as an adult because, as a social worker, I was always meeting and engaging with people in one of the most privileged ways. It is not that I went looking to gain from the professional interactions. It was sometimes unexpected when I realised that what they were saying was immediately helpful for me and my situation. Over many decades, within the confines of a professional relationship, there were nonetheless little spaces and opportunities to authentically connect with the other person. This stretched beyond roles and problems, and sometimes was transformative or healing for both myself and the client.

I have learnt and gained wisdom from clients in the sharing of their stories and challenges. It may be a by-product of their seeking help, as no-one assumed they could teach me anything. However, I think it is quite the opposite. Clients always placed themselves as the person with the problem. Somehow, they felt less than adequate because they needed help to fix the problem. While I was the social worker, the expert who could and would help. This pattern in itself was troubling. I would try to affirm people and acknowledge their strengths. However, this did not change what was a very persisting dualism of who was helping who and who the expert was. No-one saw themselves as the expert in their own lives. I would also regularly tell clients what I was learning from them. They never received it as a genuine comment.

Perhaps this seems unsurprising or nothing to worry about. The trouble is some of the most remarkable and generous gifting was from people who were in very unfree situations as involuntary clients. I have been involved in peoples' incarceration in mental health facilities, where legal coercion was used to force people with a mental illness to receive treatment against their wishes. Sometimes, I knew this intervention would not help them, and yet I still allowed it to occur. I have referred to the tyrannies that can occur in the name of care and helping. Now, to grasp the moral anguish of receiving a gift from a person who has been completely undermined by my actions is extremely hard. Hence why I have done such a substantial job at disowning the client in me. I would not want to be treated in this way. I would be devastated and traumatised.

It is probably a myth that people are helped who are placed in unfree client roles, even where there is only a minimal level of coercion. As I have mentioned, being in the client role, in and of itself, can often equate with feeling unfree. The undermining that goes with forced or coerced helping cancels out any good the helper might attempt to give. It is also a myth that only the social worker does the helping. This would have to be one of the biggest undeclared realities of the helping relationship. Clients often help the practitioner.

Within many of my helping interactions, there has been some amount of gifting by the other person towards me. Richard Titmuss famously identified the altruism of a freely given gift back in 1970. He was referring to the improved quality of a blood system in Britain based on the free-giving of blood, compared against the profit-driven system in America.4 At the interpersonal level in capitalist societies, gifting usually is tied to consumerism and the exchange of money. However, altruism is the heartbeat of all species and societies and existed long before the market economies of capitalism. Altruism could be humans being kind and generous to loved ones and strangers, and it could be other species and Nature loving us back with their gifting. I want to think about the social worker-client relationship by considering Wall Kimmerer's ideas about gifting, which draws on her Indigenous heritage as a member of the Potawatomi Nation. She explains how gifts are not so much free as they are meant to be given back to the giver in acknowledgement of reciprocity.[1] The relationship between humans and Nature – if premised on gifting as reciprocity – holds the key to mutual give-and-take without destroying Nature, the source of life.[1] For example, water is a gift from Nature, and should not be bottled and sold, or used to create Coca Cola at the expense of local springs and communities. Wall Kimmerer asks how do we find our way to recognise the planet as a gift, and thus make our relationship with Nature sacred.[1] In turn, this alerts me to the lack of reciprocity in the social worker-client relationship. In fact, it is the inequality of power in the relationship that perhaps causes harm to the client, but also a hidden loss to the social worker.

These thoughts about gifting, and how it can occur in unequal or unfree situations, bring me to the gratitude I have for clients who enact revolutionary love. I have personally experienced gifts from clients in the form of: kind words, respect, willingness to meet with me and to tell me their stories, willingness to be guided by me around intensely personal and often very painful things in their lives, and offers of their views about my work with them. The gifting of our story to another, especially if they are a stranger with the ability to exercise power over us, is truly courageous. To make ourselves that vulnerable is what Brene Brown refers to as love.[5] Clients love social workers and other helpers. Sometimes, even, when they are not being helped and not experiencing love in return. Clients have helped me tens of hundreds of times. Sometimes, I did not help the same clients back. That a person in a client role, especially as an involuntary client under state legislation, offers gifts of love is truly revolutionary. It is also, as I mentioned before, largely unrecognised. When clients love the very people who might be adding to their pain when trying to help them, it is revolutionary. It involves pivoting on broken-heartedness and turning towards love. It is love that may not be reciprocated in professionalised helping situations.

At this time, my main professional relationships are with university students, both undergraduate social work students and postgraduate students across a range of social science disciplines. The unequal power relationships have different hues, forms, and implications. But the lack of recognition of the gifting by students towards me is the same. I continue to learn so much from students in discussions with them and from reading their assignments. I like to think of myself as someone who values relationships as the place where the potential for love, learning, and healing can occur. Therefore, it is somewhat puzzling to me that I have been slow to acknowledge the hidden extent of gifting by others to me. Just as I have clung way too long to keeping my heart fortressed against intimate love with another human, so too have I clung desperately to an outmoded idea of professionalism – the expert who maintains a boundary between self and client, and who directs and even controls what counts as helping. This slowness to un-professionalise my relationships has continued at my own cost but more importantly at the cost of people with whom I engage. I need to be more willing than at previous times in my life to unpack the source of my emotional imperialism with clients and my intellectual imperialism with students. A beginning point is to reclaim my disowned client self and to reclaim my disowned student self.

This is about divesting my professional privilege, even as I exercise it with people in client or student roles. I need to invest in allowing myself the vulnerabilities that can accrue to clients and students. For example, with clients, I might be hurt by someone who is meant to help me, love me. With students, my fear is I might fail to enable social work students' learning because of my own limitations. Where my failure gets passed on to the students, who then, in turn, fail to help their future clients. This becomes a flawed type of helping that is the root cause of many clients' harm and trauma. That is, the main form of harm for clients involves the helper's emotional, and other forms of, imperialism towards them. I am working on un-professionalising how I engage with clients and students. This involves divesting of unnecessary uses of authority and claims to being an expert about what clients should do or know. Meeting clients and students as equals opens the space for a purposeful, loving relationship that serves them without hidden costs.

From bureaucratised academic to un-managing love

I highly value the opportunity academia affords me to contribute to the professional education of the next generation of social workers. I want to believe in universities as places of learning, and as places that model the best of practices, ideas, and curriculums that can make the world a better place. I have been sorely tested for holding onto this belief in universities. Universities are meant to be about creating new knowledge and educating the next generation of leaders for society across a range of disciplines. Such an honourable and important mandate. To this end, I continued to have an idealised image of the intelligentsia class – if there is such a thing. I held onto this idealism for quite some time, and longer than was wise, given what the reality was showing me. I am, these days, not willing to say there is an intelligentsia class, or at least I have unlinked being intelligent from being in academia. After witnessing some very concerning micro-aggressions in one university, an Aboriginal colleague who was new to academia said she has never seen such a mob of ego driven people in all her life. The often ruthless, extremely competitive workplace culture is not conducive to valuing differences. These differences include but are not limited to different ways of being an academic, different racial and gender identities, and, especially, different ideas. The surface veneer of polite, smart, and collaborative colleagues can sometimes hide a harsher underbelly of an individualised merit-driven system.

Nevertheless, I believe universities are potentially revolutionary places. This potential increases when academics share emancipatory (or revolutionary) ideas and research which are the currency for a peaceful and sustainable world. I became a social work academic because I wanted to believe hooks when she said that the classroom is a space of radical possibility.[6] It was an idea that led me into very troubled waters indeed. For a time, I became disillusioned of the revolutionary potential of the social work curriculum, relationships between academics and students, and classroom teaching and learning. I became constrained, and almost totally cancelled as a social work academic. This was a troubling matter for the extreme impacts it could have had on me – which, at times, were life threatening. I was bullied for so long for the ideas I was trying to live by in my teaching work. The hidden twist to the archetypal bullying story is how I engaged in a power struggle that, in part, meant I was playing the game of my academic managers. They were trying to control and manage others to agree with them and the superiority or rightness of their ideas. I would not be managed out of my ideas that I believed were morally right. This is a dimension of intellectual imperialism.

Albeit from a junior academic position, I was very determined for many years to democratise staff meetings, to actively include students in curriculum design work, to challenge unfair actions towards students, to teach in collaborative and creative ways, and to relate to students as equals in the learning journey. I was not only strongly influenced by bell hooks who promoted a relational, democratised educational approach but also by Freire. He explains that a banking approach to education regards the teacher as the expert and students as empty vessels who need filling up.[7] This did not sit well with me. I saw worrying parallels with the social worker-client relationship where professional expertism and privilege undercut the client's own knowledge and way of being. Freire wrote about how this bureaucratises people to accept the dominant views of society as the truth. This occurs even if the truth serves the elites at the expense of the public.

Initially, I did not realise there was a backlash occurring from some colleagues, due to my own experimenting with adult learning ideas and anti-oppressive ethics such as love. The educational context was not conducive to my ideas and teaching practices. The technical, instrumentalist approach to knowledge-sharing and creating has only intensified in the intervening years. I'm not sure if there has ever been academic freedom in universities, but, in my experience, the imaginative space is shrinking.[8]

My ability to practice as I felt I needed to became more and more constrained. This is what Friere would call the bureaucratisation of the mind.[7] He was referring to how we can become domesticated to dominant norms and ways, including in universities. I had to work harder to resist the backlash. I am still not sure if acting nonviolently and not retaliating in a dangerous situation will ever be enough to change interpersonal bullying that refracts broader patterns of challenge to intellectual freedom. I found small acts of resistance were dangerous. By doing my doctoral research on my teaching practice and the university context, it was perceived as a critique of senior academics. My research was threatened with legal action to try and stop the conferral of the degree. This is one poignant point where I could have been cancelled as an academic. It would have been almost impossible to come back from. The threat was multi-layered in terms of my personal safety, my job, my professional integrity, and my career. But most of all, the threat was to the ideas and values I was trying to hold on to. The ideas about love that I researched did in fact at the time, and over subsequent years, guide me in how to be a quiet, emancipatory educator. Not one with big radical curriculum approaches where I make moral demands on colleagues to agree with me. But an academic who is ever-ready to support any interested student's exploration of loving and anti-oppressive ideas and methods.

Does this mean I've sold out to the cause? I'm not sure I can truly say I was ever part of a cause for education as the practice of freedom. Or for education as the de-bureaucratisation of minds. The seriousness of this struggle for my own integrity, as I saw it, however, hides a disowned part of myself. The disowned part of me is the intellectual bully self. This is about the risk that I was mirroring the very bullying at the intellectual level that I was resisting in some of my colleagues' actions towards me. In particular, my bullying occurred towards unwilling students who may have felt trapped in my classrooms, and who had no choice but to entertain what were dangerous ideas. This danger is to be expected and needs negotiating, as it goes with the territory of challenging the status quo. The charged academic context made it literally dangerous for students to be seen to like me, or more, to like my ideas. I was placing students in a cross-current conflict that did not serve them. As just one example, many were worried they wouldn't be able to get references from senior colleagues to get employment on graduation.

Fast forward to the present time and my current role as a social work academic. My disowned intellectual bully self is perhaps even more important to take responsibility for. In a very competitive job market, it really matters to students that they have skills that employers want. That I am asking some classes to explore ideas such as love and species justice is a more sophisticated version of my earlier efforts. But how will these ideas get them jobs? While this is an ever-present awareness for me, I have worked hard at creating high quality learning materials that are relevant for students on graduation. I've also worked to create a learning space where students feel safe, respected, valued for their knowledge and experiences, and have choices on how to engage with non-traditional ideas and activities. But it is still the case that I hold authority which takes the form of marking their assessments.

I consciously work to place myself as a facilitator and colleague, not as an expert who knows more or knows better. Do I still believe the classroom can be a place to practice freedom? I am not entirely sure. It is perhaps a more conservative and more constrained learning environment than twenty years ago. Do I think it is a place to explore ideas such as love and nonviolence that inform all the great socio-environmental movements of our time? Most definitely. Can these ideas guide students in their future practice in a myriad of different contexts? It has to be so, doesn't it? The onus is on me to translate big ideas into feasible strategies and ethically nuanced actions that can enable loving, anti-oppressive practices. Only then will students see the relevance for their future practice as social workers. This is a key dedication for me at this time. I am hoping it dilutes the urge to intellectually pressure, and perhaps even bully students to accept my ideas. But I cannot be sure it is enough. This is a deep worry for me and it sits right beside my disowned self as a student. I am aware of an unwillingness to place myself in formal educational situations as a student. Because I do not like being told what to think.

In the process of writing this personal essay, I have come to recognise another disowned part of myself. As an academic, I have disowned my unintelligent self. This has been hidden by the shame of growing up poor, which included feeling shamed for not being smart. We were ordinary, struggling country folks, with no intellectuals in the family according to society's definition. My father was good with his hands. My mother was good at caring for her big family. Us kids got unremarkable school reports. No-one expected the girls to go to university. University was not a word ever used in our family. We couldn't afford to go even if we wished. The boys were to get a trade. No-one was encouraged to dream big, to invest in making smart decisions in our lives. I've carried this unnamed shame throughout my adult life. It partly accounts for my oversized sense of responsibility in my career to make a difference. Shaming hurts tremendously. Shaming can be a great motivator to avoid more of it. I need to take responsibility for my disowned intellectual bully self, that is fuelled by a fear of being regarded as unintelligent. I have to recognise in myself a type of defensive anti-authorianism towards senior colleagues where I find myself disagreeing with them and only willing to cooperate with their ideas up to a point. I was presuming to know what was best for how social work staff should treat each other, how we should treat students, and what the social work curriculum should look like. Also, I was still carrying wounds arising from growing up in a domestic violence situation. I was not ever going to let anyone boss me around.

Echoes from the past finally helped me become less arrogant and less attached to the idea that I knew best. I have let go of trying to influence others beyond my immediate work role and responsibilities. Otherwise, my fear is that I will become an intellectual bully myself, and repeat the very heart-breaking cycle I became entrapped in for many years. Further, in not taking responsibility for my shamed self, I may be projecting onto others that they are unintelligent or misguided in their practice. These hardest-of-hard disowned parts of myself have been hiding all these years behind my zeal to influence my social work colleagues, staff and students alike.

Maybe, one day, the opportunity will arise where I can be a Professor of Social Work. Then I better be ready to walk my talk of loving, anti-oppressive social work. I have much to learn and unlearn in preparing myself in the meantime. Currently, my main guiding idea is that if I truly believe in the revolutionary power of love, then be it, act it, practice it. Let that love be unmanaged, unforced on others, and undefended as an abstract idea.

From privileged species to un-humanising love

Most people who know me wouldn't know that my middle name is Wyt-Lyon, pronounced white lion. I wasn't given this name at birth, my birth name was Dianne Elizabeth Youd. In my thirties, I changed the spelling of my first name to Dyann – partly because I didn't like being called Di. I changed my last name to Ross for my daughter, so both her parents had the same name as her. Needless to say my mother was not pleased that I changed my first name and tends to still call me by the name she gave me. I understand that and don't mind. But the name most important to me is Wyt-Lyon. I wanted for myself an animal name that would help guide my spiritual journey in life. In a womens' healing retreat, it became clear that white lion needed to be my name. I didn't keep it as my surname for long though, making it my middle name when I took on our family name of Ross.

The white lion is a rare and magnificent member of the lion family, heralding from Timbavati in South Africa. Almost extinct in the wild in the early 1990s, their numbers are slowly increasing due to breeding programs in zoos and some successful releases into the wild. At the time I chose the name, I did not dwell too much on its meaning. I was aware the white lion was a mother protector creature, watching out for her Kin who were under siege from human predators. That sensibility profoundly guided my role as a new mother, and being a mother remains one of my most important dedications. For this book, I've learned that, according to the local Indigenous people of Timbavati, white lions are the caretakers of their ancestors' spirits. Slang explains that, for the Shangaan People, the white lions need to be protected as family, which is as important as protecting the country.[9] White lions are thought to be white to get humans' attention, to heed both their warnings and blessings – warnings to stop harming Nature and messages of peace. Slang explains that their spiritual purpose is to remind us that it is time to lead with heart wisdom.[9]

Obviously, I am not alone in valuing this sentiment – that it is time to connect to our heart. What is interesting for me is the way Slang's words link with my middle name, and extend on my earlier sense of the spiritual and symbolic significance of the white lion. Of course, I felt broken threads in my heart recalibrating and healing. I recognised myself and stepped more surely into the world-wide movement for peace and love of Nature. But there is some regret that I have not been more, or done more, to live up to that powerful middle name. At the same time, it feels like perfect timing to energise my name as part of recognising a disowned part of myself. I've struggled to put a name to this disowned self. For want of more clarity, I'm referring to it as my disowned animality self. This disowning shows as having gained so much advantage and privilege in my life at the cost of other animals. I say this even though I am a practising vegan. But I have still used and gained from some other animals by being complicit with speciesism for many decades of my life. The main way I have been complicit is by over-identifying with being human and thereby defining myself as different from the other animals. In part, I have done this by regarding myself as an individual, unique body with all the physicality and materiality that goes with human bodies. In being preoccupied with tending to my bodily needs, I have not sufficiently invested in cultivating a multispecies spirituality. Yet my middle name was calling out to me over the years.

Willett explains that a multispecies ethics requires a subjectless identity attachment and an intersubjectivity with other beings.[10] I understand this to mean that my ethical task in addressing speciesism is that I need to learn how to un-humanise myself. Not to confuse un-humanise with dehumanise. A focus on un-humanising is not about denying my humanity, or my embodiment in human form. Rather, it is about expanding my consciousness to build enduring connections with other species – my Kin – where the physicality of our bodies is not a barrier to that connection. I am at the beginning of this journey and take inspiration from other white women who are writing about how they are receiving guidance from First Nation People.[11]

I am part of the privileged species. I've over-concerned myself with the wellbeing of humans. And so, I have not chosen to be concerned with the wellbeing of other animals and Nature to the extent I might otherwise have done. Further, my speciesism has hidden behind a sense of pride that I was vegetarian for several decades — surely that was enough. Becoming vegan finally removed me from the direct chain of demand for dairy and chicken-based products. As Alger's book taught me, though, being vegan requires something more than not eating other animals.[12] The massive animal industrial complex means there is a scale of suffering of farmed other animals that is mind-numbing and too much to think about for too long. Avoiding thinking about other animals' suffering, avoiding living near abattoirs, or not passing too closely by a butcher shop, is just self-protection. Self-protection by avoiding the harsh, desperately troubling reality is no less than what millions of other humans do everyday. As humans, we wouldn't entertain or allow the farming and slaughter of humans, would we? By virtue of existing in a human body, I am protected to some degree from being eaten by other humans. This is a significant privilege that I do not need to do anything about to benefit from.

Alger writes about the crime of animality and relates some deeply disturbing stories of other animals being tortured and killed throughout history.[12] Other animals tend to be constructed as less intelligent than humans, less capable of feelings than humans, less by virtue of being not human. This devaluing of other animals' beingness – their animality – allows the ill treatment and mass slaughter of farmed animals to be justified. The dualisms and prejudices are increasingly being challenged, but the animal industrial complex swamps any beginning sign of societal level compassion for some other animals.

I still struggle with truly and deeply accepting my own animality. I remember being fascinated by Haraway's writing when she proclaimed that we are all destined to become compost.[13] I was also somewhat aghast at thinking of my animality in this very elementary, close-to-Nature, beyond-my-human-body kind of way. I still have a long way to go to gain some amount of detachment from my carefully constructed subjectivity to accept the materiality of my beingness. Such has been my dedication to trying to accept my humanness that I missed a secret of life. The secret is that through the common bonds of animality across all species of life forms, we can know a level of connectedness. This can be the basis for energising a broad multispecies movement for the equal worth and right to love of all beings. Integral to resting in the ethics of common bonds of animality is the embracing of being good fodder for the compost bin in my backyard. I dedicate myself to learning more about how to be in the world guided by a multispecies, post-materialist ethics. Right here and now, I refuse to rest on my privilege of being human and seek ways to pivot towards a loving and just kinship with all species and Nature.

There is an interrelated additional disowned part of myself that needs teasing out as part of un-humanising love. It is going to take humans to challenge other humans who significantly contribute to the perpetuation of the animal industrial complex and the mining industry. The harmful impacts of violence on other animals' rights to live and to be free has been a concern for me. At the centre of capitalism and colonialism is the issue of the accumulation of extreme wealth by the few, at the expense of social, species, and environmental justice of the many. I state this here to not shy away from the systemic and economic inequalities, and the higher order of responsibility that accrues to government and business elites to address these inequalities.

Meanwhile, we each have our own responsibility, proportionate to our profiting from the country's natural resources and other animals. The disowned part of myself, that is perhaps the hardest of all to call to attention, is the privileges I gain from my material wealth – that is, I have disowned my materially wealthy self. This is somewhat surprising to be saying, given I grew up in poverty and I carried the stigma and shame of a working class background with me well into my adult life. One of the side effects of wanting to make a difference in the world was that I studied for and gained several degrees. As first-in-family to go to university, this was no walk in the park. But over many years, the qualifications and career as a social worker afforded me job security, and, with that, financial security. In blunt terms, I have become relatively wealthy from two main sources. The first source of wealth derives from the suffering of other people whom I engaged with in my social work career. My social work positions have afforded me good incomes, as well as valued social status and other privileges. One significant financial privilege is the accumulation of my superannuation fund. This alone is more than I need to live comfortably into very old age. Most of this wealth consists of a very generous superannuation scheme as a social work academic. In this regard, my wealth derives from educating the next generation of social workers, who will, in turn, gain financially from other peoples' suffering. The second source of my wealth relates to the dispossession of First Nation People from their lands. As a private property owner, my main wealth beyond what I need for my basic survival needs comes from owning my own home. My home is situated on the land of the Gubbi Gubbi People of the Sunshine Coast region. I have not paid any compensation to them for this enormous privilege. It was not freely given to me by them. That I have acted according to the colonialist law in buying property gives me no moral ease. For settler societies such as Australia, all non-Aboriginal people who own property are implicated in the stealing of the land and its wealth from the traditional owners.

It is deeply painful to me that every day my own wellbeing, security, and wealth can be traced back to the suffering and losses experienced by other people. I have yet to find any comfort or ways of thinking about my material wealth privileges. I try to be generous with my financial wealth. This, however, does nothing to redress the collective moral injury I am part of when I witness the ongoing trauma, prejudice, and loss of many First Nation People, including local families in my own community. With regard to gaining from the suffering of people in client roles, I can cling to the hope that I made positive contributions for some of the people. But I do not know, and can't substantiate, the value of what I have done in my professional social work role.

All I can say is that it is likely that I will continue to experience broken-heartedness for these reasons, as well as for the witnessing of trauma and loss by other animals and Nature. To not have a broken heart could mean a number of things. The worst implication for me would be that I have become hard-hearted and simply do not care anymore. I am an unfinished moral project, and in saying this, I am not trying to excuse myself from my proper responsibilities.

Postscript

ON THE 14TH of October, 2023, Australians voted in the Voice Referendum. In a book that bears witness to broken-heartedness, the last words are provided by Thomas Mayo who continues to lead with his words, against the terrible, soul-wrenching loss of the yes vote. On October the 21st, he writes:

In the week of silence, I have had time to reflect on last Saturday's outcome, I have concluded Indigenous Peoples were correct to take the invitation in the Uluru Statement from the Heart to the Australian people. We were not wrong to ask them to recognise us through a Voice.

For a people with inherent rights but who are a minority spread across this vast continent - with a parliament that will continue to make laws and policies about us - it is inevitable that we will need to establish a national representative body to pursue justice. [...]

As a leader of the campaign, I accept that, although we tried our best, we failed. [...] These thoughts hurt, like an aching emptiness in my chest. [...]

The heart of the nation is still here. It always was and it always will be, waiting to be recognised by our fellow

Australians. Whether you voted 'yes' or 'no', I say to you with humility and respect, open your hearts and your minds henceforth.

The truth should be unifying, not divisive.[1]

References

Acknowledgement

[1] Mayo, T. (2023, April 15). *The right side of history*. The Saturday Paper, 7.

Lovelessness

[1] Richardson, L. (2000). Writing: A method of inquiry. In N. Denzin & Y. Lincoln (Eds.). *Handbook of qualitative research* (2nd ed., pp. 923–948). Sage Publications.

[2] Ellis, C., & Flaherty, M. (Eds.). (1992). *Investigating subjectivity: Research on lived experience*. Sage Publications.

[3] Ellis, C. (1997). Writing emotionally about our lives. In W. Tierney & Y. Lincoln (Eds.). *Representation and the text: Re-framing the narrative voice* (pp. 115–138). State University of New York Press.

[4] hooks, b. (2000). *Feminism is for everybody: Passionate politics*. Pluto Press.

[5] From the heart (2022). *What is constitutional recognition through a voice to parliament?* https://australianstogether.org.au/other-resources/voice-to-parliament/#:~:text=A%20constitutionally%20enshrined%20Voice%20would,that%20

impact%20First%20Nations%20people.

[6] United Nations. (1989, November 20). *The convention on the rights of the child.* https://www.ohchr.org/en/instruments-mechanisms/instruments convention-rights-child

[7] hooks, b. (2001a). *All about love: New visions.* William Morrow.

[8] hooks, b. (1995). *Killing rage: Ending racism.* Henry Holt & Company.

[9] Freire, P. (1970). *Pedagogy of the oppressed.* Herder & Herder.

Violence

[1] Strauss, E., Curley, J., Shizuka, D., & Hobson, E. (2022). The centennial of the pecking order: Current state and future prospects for the study of dominance hierarchies. Philosophical Transactions of the Royal Society Series B. *Biological Sciences, 377*(1845), 20200432–20200432. http://doi.org/10.1098/rstb.2020.0432

[2] Orwell, G. (1944). *Animal farm.* The Text Publishing Company.

[3] Young, I. (1990). *Justice and the politics of difference.* Princeton University Press.

[4] Gillespie, G., Grubb, P., Brown, K., Boesch, M., & Ulrich, D. (2017). "Nurses eat their young": A novel bullying educational program for student nurses. *Journal of Nursing Education and Practice, 7*(11), 11–21. https://doi.org/10.5430/jnep.v7n7P11

[5] Thompson, N. (2017). *Promoting equality: Challenging discrimination and oppression* (4th ed.). Bloomsbury Academic.

6 Palmer, M., & Ross, D. (2014). Tracing the maddening effects of abuses of authority: Rationalities gone violent in mental health services and universities. *Social Alternatives, 33*(3), 28–36.

7 Goffman, E. (1961). *Asylums: Essays on the social situation of mental patients and other inmates.* Anchor Books.

8 Kemble, R. (2014). The intolerable taboo of mental illness. *Social Alternatives, 33*(3), 20–23.

9 Quitangon, G. (2019). Vicarious trauma in clinicians: Fostering resilience and preventing burn out. *Psychiatric Times, 36*(7), 18–19.

10 Clement, S., Schauman, O., Graham, T., Maggioni, F., Evans-Lacko, S., Bezborodovs, N., Morgan, C., Rusch, N., Brown, J., & Thornicroft, G. (2015). What is the impact of mental health-related stigma on help-seeking? A systematic literature review on quantitative and qualitative studies. *Psychological Medicine, 45*(1), 11–27.

11 Kesey, K. (1962). *One flew over the cuckoo's nest.* Penguin.

12 Forman, M. (Director). (1975). *One flew over the cuckoo's nest.* [Film]. United Films.

13 Victorian Royal Commission (2021). *Royal commission into Victoria's mental health system.* https://finalreport.rcvmhs.vic.gov.au/

14 Barnett, B. (2020). Addressing sexual violence in psychiatric facilities. *Psychiatric Services, 71*(9), 959–961. https://doi.org/10.1176/appi.ps.202000038

15 Clarke, K., Barnes, M., & Ross, D. (2018). I had no other option: Women, ECT and informed consent. *Journal of Mental Health Nursing, 27*(3), 1077–1085.

16 Ross, D. (2020). Towards coercion free, trauma-informed care

in Australian adult mental health services: Strategies for social workers. *Social Work and Mental Health, 18*(5), 536-553.

[17] Ross, D., Campbell, J., & Dyer, A. (2014). Fostering trauma-free mental health workplace cultures and reducing seclusion and restraint. *Social Alternatives, 33*(3), 37–45.

[18] Morton, R. (2023, April 15). Mental Health Commission in crisis. *The Saturday Paper*, 1–6.

[19] Aubusson, K. (2017, May 12). Naked, drugged and secluded: "Horrific" footage of patient's death at Lismore Base Hospital sparks statewide investigation. *The Sydney Morning Herald*. http://www.smh.com.au/video/video-news/video-nsw-news/naked-drugged-and-secluded-20170512-4twik.html

[20] Wright, M. (2017). *Review of seclusion, restraint and observation of consumers with a mental illness in NSW Health facilities*. https://www.health.nsw.gov.au/mentalhealth/reviews/seclusionprevention/Documents/report-seclusion-restraint-observation.pdf

[21] Bloom, S. (2017). The sanctuary model: Through the lens of moral safety. In S. Gold (Ed.). *APA handbook of trauma psychology: Trauma practice* (pp. 499–513). American Psychological Association. https://doi.org/10.1037/0000020-024

[22] Mendez, J. (2013, March 5). *When a health carer becomes a torturer. Key report by the UN Special Rapporteur on torture*. https://www.ohchr.org/en/press-releases/2013/03/when-health-carer-becomes-torturer-key-report-un-special-rapporteur-torture

[23] United Nations (2010). *Interpretation of torture in the light of*

the practice and jurisprudence of international bodies. https://www.ohchr.org/sites/default/files/Documents/Issues/Torture/UNVFVT/Interpretation_torture_2011_EN.pdf

[24] QHealth (2023). *Mental Health Act 2016 chief psychiatrist policy.* https://www.health.qld.gov.au/__data/assets/pdf_file/0025/465163/cpp-seclusion.pdf

[25] De Cuyper, K., Vanlinthout, E., Vanhoof, J., van Achterberg, T., Opgenhaffen, T., Nijs, S., Peeters, T., Put, J., Maes, B., & Van Audenhove, C. (2023). Best practice recommendations on the application of seclusion and restraint in mental health services: An evidence, human rights and consensus-based approach. *Journal of psychiatric and mental health nursing, 30*(3), 580–593. https://doi.org/10.1111/jpm.12890

Eco Injustice

[1] The term Nature is often used instead of the environment or the natural environment. It always means to include people and other animals. These are given their own category when considered matters of justice or when an emphasis is wanted on one of all three dimensions of Nature – people, other animals and the environment.

[2] World Wildlife Fund (2022). *Living planet report.* https://wwf.org.au/what-we-do/living-planet-report/#gs.voe3k4

[3] Australian Koala Foundation (2020). *Threats to the koala.* https://www.savethekoala.com/about-koalas/threats-to-the-koala/

[4] Ruiz, A. (2023). *How many trees are cut down every day?* https://theroundup.org/

how-many-trees-are-cut-down-every-day/

[5] Australia Institute of Health and Safety, (2021, July 2). *Black lung disease on the rise: Safe Work Australia.* https://www.aihs.org.au/news-and-publications/news/black-lung-disease-rise-safe-work-australia

[6] Shan, H., Chen, H., Harvey, M., Stemn, E., & Cliff, D. (2018). Focusing on coal workers' lung diseases: A comparative analysis of China, Australia, and the United States. *International Journal of Environmental Research and Public Health, 15*(11), 2565. https://doi.org/10.3390/ijerph15112565

[7] Santini, T. (2022). Opening up WA's options for mine closures. In S. Saggar, R. Rey & C. Lin (Eds.), *WA 2050: People, place and prosperity* (p. 51). UWA Public Policy Institute.

[8] Asare, B., Robinson, S., Powell, D., & Kwanicka, D. (2023). Health and related behaviours of fly-in fly-out workers in the mining industry in Australia: A cross-sectional study. *International Archives of Occupational and Environmental Health, 96*(1), 105–120. https://doi.org/10.1007/s00420-022-01908-x

[9] Turner, J. (2015, March 10). *Fly-in, fly-out – the mental and physical effects of mining work schedules.* Mining Technology. https://www.mining-technology.com/features/featureon-the-fly-the-mental-and-physical-effects-of-fifo-work-schedules1-4521166/

[10] Soderbergh, S. (Director). (2000). *Erin Brokovich.* [Film]. Universal Pictures.

[11] Steinberg, J. (2013, July 9). *Hinkley: No Hollywood ending for town plagued by toxic water.* Daily Breeze. https://www.dailybreeze.com/2013/07/09/hinkley-

no-hollywood-ending-for-town-plagued-by-toxic-water/

[12] Sharp, C. (2004). *Report for the standing committee on environment and public affairs in relation to the Alcoa refinery at Wagerup inquiry.* Government of Western Australia.

[13] Brueckner, M., & Ross, D. (2010). *Under corporate skies: A struggle between people, place and profit.* Fremantle Press.

[14] You might be interested to look at the extensive material and stories provided by Community Alliance for Positive Solutions (CAPS), Yarloop's remaining activist group's website: https://caps6218.org.au/

[15] This initiative was called the Bucket Brigade and consisted of locals going to locations where there was a pollution event and using a specially designed bucket to capture the air.

[16] See details on CAPS website: https://caps6218.org.au/

[17] Ferguson, E. (2016). *Report of the special inquiry into the January 2016 Waroona fire.* Government of Western Australia.

[18] Milne, P. (2023, February 15). *Alcoa's deal with WA a 62-year-old relic from a different time.* WA Today. https://www.watoday.com.au/environment/sustainability/alcoa-s-deal-with-wa-a-62-year-old-relic-from-a-different-time-20230214-p5ckfs.html

[19] Carson, R. (1962). *Silent spring.* Penguin.

[20] Gore, A. (2007). *An inconvenient truth: The crisis of global warming.* Viking Books.

[21] Boetto, H. (2019). Advancing transformative eco-social change: Shifting from modernist to holistic foundations. *Australian Social Work, 72*(2), 139–152.

[22] Laville, S. (2020, December 10). Human-made materials now

outweigh Earth's entire biomass – study. *The Guardian.*
https://www.theguardian.com/environment/2020/dec/09/
human-made-materials-now-outweigh-earths-entire-
biomass-study

[23] Hines, A. (2023, May 10). *Decade of defiance: Ten years of
reporting land and environmental activism worldwide.*
https://www.globalwitness.org/en/campaigns/
environmental-activists/decade-defiance/

[24] Dusevic, T. (2023, January 28–29). 411.5bn boost for budget
recovery. *The Weekend Australian.*

[25] Langenberg, A. (2022, June 24). *Tasmania's
upper house effectively passes legislation
to impose harsher penalties on protesters.* ABC
News. https://www.abc.net.au/news/2022-06-24/
anti-protest-laws-a-step-closer-in-tasmania/101173690

[26] Cleary, P. (2012). *Mine-field: The dark side of Australia's
resources rush.* Black Ink Books.

[27] Woodley, M. (2020). The wrong side of Native title, the
right side of mining. In D. Ross, M. Brueckner, M. Palmer
& W. Eaglehawk (Eds.), *Eco-activism and social work: New
directions in leadership and group work* (pp. 61–73).
Routledge.

[28] Cleary, P. (2021). *Title fight: How the Yindjibarndi battled and
defeated a mining giant.* Black Ink Books.

[29] Wooltorton, S., Poelina, A., & Collard, L. (2021). River
relationships: For the love of rivers. *River Research and
Applications, 38*(3), 393–403.

[30] Poelina, A. (2020). First law is the natural law of the land.
In D. Ross., M. Brueckner, M. Palmer & W. Eaglehawk (Eds.),
Eco-activism and social work: New directions in leadership

and group work (pp. viii-xii). Routledge.

[31] Andre, J. (2023, June 29). *Global ambition for renewable energy drives critical minerals boom, but new mines years away.* ABC News. https://www.abc.net.au/news/2023-06-29/queensland-critical-minerals-boom-but-new-mines-years-away/102535094

[32] Thompson, B., & Packham, C. (2022, December 7). Andrew Forrest is Australia's biggest renewables player. *Australian Financial Review.* https://www.afr.com/companies/energy/andrew-forrest-s-squadron-energy-seals-4b-deal-for-cwp-renewables-20221207-p5c4dv

[33] Shepherd, T. (2022, March 27). "Judge me on my actions": Can Andrew Forrest become Australia's clean green hero? *The Guardian.* https://www.theguardian.com/australia-news/2022/mar/27/judge-me-on-my-actions-can-andrew-forrest-become-australias-clean-green-hero

[34] Slezak, M. (2016, March 3). Coalmines could wipe out threatened black-throated finch habitat – study. *The Guardian.* https://www.theguardian.com/australia-news/2016/mar/03/coalmines-could-wipe-out-threatened-black-throated-finch-habitat-study

[35] Wangan Jagalingou (2020, April 25). *Adani relies on draconian laws to deny Aboriginal rights.* https://wanganjagalingou.com.au/adani-relies-on-draconian-laws-to-deny-aboriginal-rights/

[36] Smee, B. (2020, August 24). Access to Adani's Carmichael coalmine in Queensland blocked by traditional owners. *The Guardian.* https://www.theguardian.com/environment/2020/aug/24/adanis-carmichael-coalmine-in-queensland-blocked-by-traditional-owners

[37] Wangan Jagalingou (2020, February 6). *If they destroy our country, they will destroy us as a people.* https://wanganjagalingou.com.au/if-they-destroy-our-country-they-will-destroy-us-as-a-people/

[38] Woodley, M., & Ross, D. (2021). First Nation leaders' lessons on sustainability and the environment for social work. In B. Bennett (Ed.), *Aboriginal fields of practice* (pp. 216–228). Red Globe Press.

[39] Gergis, J. (2023, July 1-7). El Nino's menace. *The Saturday Paper*, 7.

[40] Brookes, S. (2022, March 24). *Last remaining Wittenoom properties to be demolished in bid to deter danger seeking tourists.* WA Today. https://www.watoday.com.au/national/western-australia/last-remaining-wittenoom-properties-to-be-demolished-in-bid-to-deter-danger-seeking-tourists-20220324-p5a7ju.html

[41] Knaus, C. (2017, October 9). Australian defence force warned about toxic firefighting foam 30 years ago. *The Guardian.* https://www.theguardian.com/australia-news/2017/oct/09/australian-defence-force-warned-about-toxic-firefighting-foam-30-years-ago

[42] The Sydney Morning Herald (2020, March 4). Justice at last for those affected by military's toxic fire retardant. *The Sydney Morning Herald.* https://www.smh.com.au/politics/nsw/justice-at-last-for-those-affected-by-military-s-toxic-fire-retardant-20200304-p546v3.html

[43] Wahlquist, C., & Allam, L. (2020, December 9). Juukan Gorge inquiry into Rio Tinto's decision to blow up Indigenous rock shelters inexcusable. *The Guardian.* https://www.

theguardian.com/australia-news/2020/dec/09/juukan-gorge-inquiry-rio-tintos-decision-to-blow-up-indigenous-rock-shelters-inexcusable

[44] Kelly, J. (2007, January 13). Day the birds fell dead. *The Sunday Times.*

[45] De Kruijff, P. (2022, May 3). Mines clear more trees than logging in WA's threatened forests. *The Sydney Morning Herald.* https://www.smh.com.au/environment/conservation/bauxite-mining-clearing-more-trees-than-loggers-in-wa-s-threatened-jarrah-forests-20220502-p5ahrt.html

[46] Environmental Protection Authority, EPA (2003). *Ludlow titanium minerals mine, 34 kilometres south of Bunbury.* https://www.epa.wa.gov.au/sites/default/files/EPA_Report/1621_B1098.pdf

[47] WA Forest Alliance, Wilderness Society & Conservation Council of WA (2022). *A thousand cuts: Mining in the northern jarrah forest.* https://wafa.org.au/wp-content/uploads/2022/05/A-Thousand-Cuts-NJF-Report-FINAL.pdf

[48] Haraway, D. (2008). *When species meet.* University of Minnesota.

[49] Eaglehawk, W. (2020). Species justice is for everybody. In D. Ross, M. Brueckner, M. Palmer & W. Eaglehawk (Eds.). *Eco-activism and social work: New directions in leadership and group work* (pp. 100-110). Routledge.

[50] Greer, G. (1993). *The female eunuch.* Flamingo.

[51] Britannica (2023). *A contribution to the critique of political economy.* https://www.britannica.com/topic/A-Contribution-to-the-Critique-of-Political-Economy

[52] Mies, M., & Shiva, V. (1993). *Ecofeminism.* Zed Books.

[53] Lyall, S. (1997, June 22). Her majesty's court has ruled: McDonald's burgers are not poison. *The New York Times*. https://www.nytimes.com/1997/06/22/weekinreview/her-majesty-s-court-has-ruled-mcdonald-s-burgers-are-not-poison.html

[54] Ritzer, G. (2000). *The McDonaldization of society*. Sage.

[55] Nagesh, A. (2017, December 31). *The harrowing psychological toll of slaughterhouse work*. https://metro.co.uk/2017/12/31/how-killing-animals-everyday-leaves-slaughterhouse-workers-traumatised-7175087/

[56] Fraser, H., & Taylor, N. (2021). Animals as domestic violence victims: A challenge to humanist social work. In V. Bozalek & Pease, B. (Eds.), *Post-anthropocentric social work: Critical posthuman and new materialist perspectives* (pp. 161–174). Routledge.

[57] Coulter, K. (2016). *Animals, work, and the promise of interspecies solidarity*. Palgrave Macmillan.

[58] Alger, K. (2020). *Five essays for freedom: A political primer for animal advocates*. Revolutionaries.

[59] Rinehart, G. (2016). *Gina Rinehart reveals her landholdings*. https://www.hancockprospecting.com.au/wp-content/uploads/2017/02/Gina-Rinehart-reveals-her-landholdings.pdf

[60] Rinehart, G. (2022). *60th Australian Export Awards winner | 2GR Wagyu from Aussie paddocks to plates across the planet*. https://www.ginarinehart.com.au/60th-australian-export-awards-winner-2gr-wagyu-from-aussie-paddocks-to-plates-across-the-planet/

[61] Neales, S. (2017, May 15). Andrew Forrest's beef with Gina Rinehart's cattle export plans. *Weekly Times Now*. https://

www.weeklytimesnow.com.au/agribusiness/cattle/andrew-forrests-beef-with-gina-rineharts-cattle-export-plans/news-story/0731c40f5bf60652d712b8df5747f288

[62] Osborne, H., & van der Zee, B. (2020, January 20). Live export: Animals at risk giant global industry. *The Guardian*. https://www.theguardian.com/environment/2020/jan/20/live-export-animals-at-risk-as-giant-global-industry-goes-unchecked

[63] Laurie, V. (2019, May 4-5). Alive and kicking. *The Weekend Australian Magazine*, 30–33.

[64] Wahlquist, C. (2023, March 3). Australia to phase out live sheep export amid opposition from peak farmers body. *The Guardian*. https://www.theguardian.com/australia-news/2023/mar/03/australia-to-phase-out-live-sheep-export-amid-opposition-from-peak-farmers-body#:~:text=Mussell%20said%20the%20live%20sheep,opinion%20were%20against%20the%20trade.

Broken-heartedness

[1] Freire, P. (1970). *Pedagogy of the oppressed*. Herder and Herder.

[2] Clarke, K., Barnes, M., & Ross, D. (2018). I had no other option: Women, ECT and informed consent. *Journal of Mental Health Nursing, 27*(3), 1077–1085.

[3] Vocabulary.com (2022). *Brokenheartedness*. https://www.vocabulary.com/dictionary/brokenheartedness

[4] Goodreads (2023). *Broken hearts book list*. https://www.goodreads.com/list/tag/broken-heart

[5] The New York Times (2022). *Books for broken*

hearts. https://www.nytimes.com/2019/02/13/books/
books-for-broken-hearts.html

6 Inglis, T. (2013). *Love.* Routledge.

7 Winch, G. (2018). *How to fix a broken heart.* [Audiobook].
Simon & Schuster.

8 Scholz, M. (2019). Learning how to heal a broken heart.
Independently published.

9 Banson, R. (2019). *Healing for the broken hearted.* Booklocker.
com

9 Walton, J., & Galland, S. (2022). *Moving forward from a broken
heart (for men) and finding the perfect partner.* [Audiobook].
Amazon Audible.

10 Mills, C. W. (1959). *The sociological imagination.* Oxford
University Press.

11 Cancer Council of Australia (2023, April). *Cancer council
Australia.* https://www.healthdirect.gov.au/partners/
cancer-council-australia

12 Sexton, E. (2007, November 27). Bernie Banton 1946–2007.
The Sydney Morning Herald. https://www.smh.com.au/
national/bernie-banton-1946-2007-20071127-gdrozn.html

13 Thomashow, M. (2014, December 19). *What is the ecological
imagination?* https://www.mitchellthomashow.com/blog/
what-is-the-ecological-imagination

14 Goodall, J., & Abrams, D. (2021). *The book of hope: A survival
guide for an endangered planet.* Penguin Random House.

15 Phys.org (2019, January 14). *Million dead fish cause
environmental stink in Australia.* https://phys.org/
news/2019-01-million-dead-fish-environmental-australia.
html

16 Morton, A. (2023, March 17). 'Unfathomable': Millions of

dead fish blanket river near Menindee in latest mass kill. *The Guardian.* https://www.theguardian.com/australia-news/2023/mar/17/unfathomable-millions-of-dead-fish-blanket-river-near-menindee-in-latest-mass-kill

[17] Visona, S., Villani, S., Manzoni, F., Chen, Y., Ardissino G., Russo, F., Moretti, M., Javan, G., & Osculati, A. (2018). Impact of asbestos on public health: A retrospective study on a series of subjects with occupational and non-occupational exposure to asbestos during the activity of Fibronit plan (Broni, Italy). *Journal of Public Health Research, 7*(3), 1519.

[18] Clarke, B., Otto, F., Stuart-Smith, R., & Harrington, L. (2022). Extreme weather impacts of climate change: An attribution perspective. *Environmental Research: Climate, 1*(1), 1–25.

[19] Noble, C. (2021). Ecofeminism to feminist materialism: Implications for Anthropocene feminist social work. In Bozalek, V. & Pease, B. (Eds.), *Post-anthropocentric social work: Critical posthuman and new materialist perspectives* (pp. 95–107). Routledge.

[20] Smith, D. (1990). *The conceptual practices of power: A feminist sociology of knowledge.* Northeastern University Press.

[21] Simard, S. (2022). *Finding the mother tree: Uncovering the wisdom and intelligence of the forest.* Penguin Books.

[22] Resnick, H., Acierno, R., & Kilpatrick, D. (2010). Health impact of interpersonal violence 2: Medical and mental health outcomes. *Behavioural Medicine, 23*(2), 65–78.

[23] LeWine, H. (2023, June, 13). *Takotsubo cardiomyopathy, broken heart syndrome.* https://www.health.harvard.edu/heart-health/takotsubo-cardiomyopathy-broken-heart-syndrome

[24] Shayne, T. (2019, October 2017). *Broken heart syndrome: Can you live with a broken heart?* https://www.gaia.com/article/broken-heart-syndrome-can-you-live-with-a-broken-heart

[25] Mazza, M., Marano, G., del Castillo, A. G., Chieffo, D., Albano, G., Biondi-Zoccai, G., Galiuto, L., Sani, G., & Romagnoli, E. (2021). Interpersonal violence: Serious sequelae for heart disease in women. *World Journal of Cardiology, 13*(9), 438–445. https://doi.org/10.4330/WJC.V13.I9.438

[26] Australian Bureau of Statistics.(2022, August 24). *3.6 million people experienced partner emotional abuse.* https://www.abs.gov.au/media-centre/media-releases/36-million-people-experienced-partner-emotional-abuse

[27] Sloan-Lynch, J. (2012). Domestic abuse as terrorism. *Hypatia: A Journal of Feminist Philosophy, 27*(4), 774–790. https://doi.org/10.1111/j.1527-2001.2011.01250.x

[28] Braden, G. (2015). *Resilience from the heart: The power to thrive in life's extremes.* Hay House Inc.

[29] Sgoifo, A., Montano, N., Esler, M., & Vaccarino, V. (2017). Stress, behaviour and the heart. *Neuroscience and Biobehavioral Reviews, 74*(Pt B), 257–259. doi: 10.1016/j.neubiorev.2016.11.003.

[30] Better Health (2022, September 8). Heart disease and mental health. https://www.betterhealth.vic.gov.au/health/healthyliving/heart-disease-and-mental-health

[31] Walker, H. (2015, October 16). George Bender dies of a "broken heart", says family. *Brisbane Times.* http://www.brisbanetimes.com.au/queensland/george-bender-died-of-a-broken-heart-says-family-20151016-gkazbp.html#ixzz3ojBbzCfB

[32] Buber, M. (1970). *I and Thou.* (Trans. W. Kaufmann).

Simon & Schuster.

[33] Abuelaish, I. (2012). *I shall not hate*. Bloomsbury.

[34] Adams, M. (2023, April 4). *Eco-anxiety: Climate change affects our mental health – here's how to cope*. The Conversation. https://theconversation.com/eco-anxiety-climate-change-affects-our-mental-health-heres-how-to-cope-202477

Love

[1] hooks, b. (1994). *Teaching to transgress: Education as the practice of freedom*. Routledge.

[2] hooks, b. (2001). *Salvation: Black people and love*. William Morrow.

[3] hooks, b. (2001). *All about love: New visions*. William Morrow.

[4] Freire, P. (1997). *Pedagogy of the heart*. Continuum.

[5] Peck, S, (1978). *The road less travelled: A new psychology of love, traditional values and spiritual growth*. Arrow Books.

[6] Fromm, E. (1956). *The art of loving*. Harper & Row.

[7] Mayman, J. (2002, May 11–12). The stink of Uncle Al. *The Weekend Australian*, 19.

[8] Brueckner, M., & Ross, D. (2010). *Under corporate skies: A struggle between people, place and profit*. Fremantle Press.

[9] Boochani, B. (2019). *No friends but the mountain: Writing from Manus prison*. (O. Tofighian, Trans.). Picador Australia.

[10] Guardian staff (2019, August 12). Behrouz Boochani wins National Biography award – and accepts via WhatsApp from Manus. *The Guardian*. https://www.theguardian.com/books/2019/aug/12/behrouz-boochani-wins-25000-national-biography-award-and-accepts-via-whatsapp-from-manus

[11] Lukes, S. (1974). *Power: A radical view.* Macmillan.

[12] cited in Seidman, S. (2016). *Contested knowledges: Social theory today* (6th ed.). Wiley-Blackwell.

[13] Foucault, M. (1980). *Power/knowledge: Selected interviews and other writings, 1972-1977.* (C. Gordon, Trans.). Harvester Press.

[14] Mills, C. W. (1956). *The power elite.* Oxford University Press.

[15] Foucault, M. (1977). *Discipline and punish: The birth of the prison.* Pantheon Books.

[16] Smith, D. (1990). *The conceptual practices of power: A feminist sociology of knowledge.* Northeastern University Press.

[17] Newell, K (2018, July). *Casenote: Doctors for refugees case.* Kaldor Centre. https://kaldorcentre.unsw.edu.au/sites/kaldorcentre.unsw.edu.au/files/Casenote_doctors%20case-final.pdf

[18] Goffman, E. (1986). *Stigma: Notes on the management of spoiled identity.* Touchstone.

[19] Szasz, T. (1972). *The myth of mental illness.* Harper & Row.

[20] Hanh, T. (1997). *True love: A practice for awakening the heart.* Shambala.

[21] Burke, T., & Brown, B. (Eds.). (2021). *You are your best thing: Vulnerability, shame resilience, and the Black experience.* Vermilion Books.

[22] hooks, b. (1995). *Killing rage: Ending racism.* Henry Holt & Company.

[23] Pease, B., Vreugdenhil, A., & Stanford, S. (Eds.). (2018). *Critical ethics of care in social work: Transforming the politics and practices of caring.* Routledge.

[24] British Medical Association (2022). *Vicarious trauma: Signs and strategies for coping.* https://www.bma.org.

uk/advice-and-support/your-wellbeing/vicarious-trauma/
vicarious-trauma-signs-and-strategies-for-coping

[25] Queensland Government (2022, September 23). *Work health and safety laws.* https://www.worksafe.qld.gov.au/ laws-and-compliance/work-health-and-safety-laws

[26] Thompson, N. (2017). *Promoting equality: Challenging discrimination and oppression* (4th ed.). Bloomsbury Academic.

[27] Bloom, S. (2013). *Creating sanctuary: Toward the evolution of sane societies.* Routledge.

[28] Macy, J. (1984). *Despair and personal power in the nuclear age.* New Society Publishers.

[29] Brown, M. (2020, June 18). *Joanna Macy – befriending your despair.* https://workthatreconnects.org/resource/ joanna-macy-befriending-your-despair/

[30] Haraway, D. (2008). *When species meet.* University of Minnesota.

[31] Stanfield, E. (2021). *Black Lives Matter in Australia: First Nation perspectives.* https://newsroom.unsw.edu.au/news/ business-law/black-lives-matter-movement-australia-first-nations-perspectives

[32] Jackson, F. (2020, September 25). *The real influencers – bell hooks.* Daily Sundial. https://sundial.csun.edu/160736/ watch/the-real-influencers-bell-hooks/

[33] Supernegromagic. (2011, April 18). *Cornel West: Justice is what love looks like in public.* [Video]. YouTube. https:// www.youtube.com/watch?v=nGqP7S_WO6o

[34] Laurie, T., & Stark, H. (2015, September, 24). *How to do politics with love.* [Conference Paper]. Capitalism and Schizophrenia: Conference for the Cluster

for Organizations Society and Markets (COSM), Melbourne, Australia. https://www.researchgate.net/publication/282652827_How_To_Do_Politics_With_Love

[35] Dryzek, J. (1990). *Discursive democracy: Politics, policy and political science.* Cambridge University Press.

[36] Kars, I. (2020, October 16). Closing the gap 12 years on: Little progress, high hopes. *National Indigenous Times.* https://nit.com.au/16-10-2020/1458/closing-the-gap-12-years-on-little-progress-high-hopes

[37] Ross, D. (2018). A social work perspective on seclusion and restraint in Australia's public mental health system. *Journal of Progressive Human Services: Radical Thought and Praxis, 29*(1), 1–19. https://doi.org/10.1080/10428232.2018.1442972

[37] Ross, D. (2020). Towards coercion free, trauma-informed care in Australian adult mental health services: *Strategies for social workers. Social Work and Mental Health, 18*(5), 536–553.

Nonviolence

[1] Attenborough, R.(Director). (1982). *Gandhi.* [Film]. Goldcrest Films.

[2] Delhi News, (2010, July 22). Mahatma Gandhi's long-forgotten diary recovered. *Hindustan Times.* https://www.hindustantimes.com/delhi/mahatma-gandhi-s-long-forgotten-diary-recovered/story-kVlz5UfO51nJj5m31J1BQM.html

[3] Sethia, T., & Narayan, A. (Eds.). (2013). *The living Gandhi: Lessons for our times.* Penguin Books.

[4] Biswas, S. (2015, September 17). *Was Mahatma Gandhi racist?* BBC News Service. https://www.bbc.com/news/world-asia-india-34265882

[5] Gandhi, R. (2013). Gandhi's journey to Ahimsa. In T. Sethia & A. Narayan (Eds.), *The living Gandhi: Lessons of our times* (pp. 101-117). Penguin.

[6] Gandhi, M. (1928). *Satyagraha in South Africa.* Jitendra T. Desai Navajivan Publishing House. https://www.mkgandhi.org/ebks/satyagraha_in_south_africa.pdf

[7] Sharp, G. (1973). *198 methods of nonviolent direct action.* Albert Einstein Institution. https://www.brandeis.edu/peace-conflict/pdfs/198-methods-non-violent-action.pdf

[8] Chenoweth, E. (2021). *Civil resistance: What everyone needs to know.* Oxford University Press.

[9] The King Centre (2022). *Dr King's fundamental philosophy of nonviolence.* https://thekingcenter.org/about-tkc/the-king-philosophy/

[10] hooks, b. (2001). *All about love: New visions.* William Morrow.

[11] Canadian Counselling and Psychotherapy Association (2020). *Code of ethics.* https://www.ccpa-accp.ca/wp-content/uploads/2020/05/CCPA-2020-Code-of-Ethics-E-Book-EN.pdf

[12] Bloom, S. (2013). *Creating sanctuary: Toward the evolution of sane societies.* Routledge.

[13] Sanctuary Institute (2022). *The sanctuary model.* https://www.thesanctuaryinstitute.org/about-us/the-sanctuary-model/

[14] Hem, M., Gjerberg, E., Husum, T., & Pedersen, R. (2018). Ethical challenges when using coercion in mental health care: A systematic review. *Nursing Ethics, 25*(1), 92–110.

[15] The Australian Human Rights Commission (1997, April).

Bringing them home report: Report of the National Inquiry into the Separation of Aboriginal and Torres Strait Islander Children from Their Families. https://humanrights.gov.au/our-work/bringing-them-home-report-1997

[16] Bennett, B. (2019). The importance of Aboriginal history for practitioners. In B. Bennett & S. Green (Eds.). *Our voices: Aboriginal social work* (2nd ed., pp. 3–29). Red Globe Press.

[17] AIATSIS (2023, July 13). *The stolen generations.* https://aiatsis.gov.au/explore/stolen-generations

[18] Bennett, B., Green, S., Gilbert, S., & Bessarb, D. (Eds.). (2013). *Our voices: Aboriginal and Torres Strait Islander social work.* Red Globe Press.

[18] Walter, M., Taylor, S., & Habibis, D. (2019). Australian social work is white. In B. Bennett & S. Green (Eds.). *Our voices: Aboriginal social work* (2nd edn., pp. 230-244). Bloomsbury Academic.

[19] Maylea, C. (2020). *Social work and the law: A guide for ethical practice.* Red Globe Press.

[20] Russo, J., & Sweeney, A. (Eds.). (2016). *Searching for a rose garden: Challenging psychiatry, fostering mad studies.* PCCS Book Ltd.

[21] Eaglehawk, W. (2020). Species justice is for everybody. In D. Ross, M. Brueckner, M. Palmer & W. Eaglehawk (Eds.). *Eco-activism and social work: New directions in leadership and group work* (pp. 100–110). Routledge.

[22] Andres, J., Verzier, M., & Peitrouisti, L. (Eds.). (2021). *More-than-human.* The Nieuwe Institute.

[23] Alger, K. (2020). *Five essays for freedom: A political primer for animal advocates.* Revolutionaries.

[24] Singer, P. (1975). *Animal liberation: A new ethics for our*

treatment of animals. Harper Collins.

[25] Francione, G., & Charlton, A. (2013). *Animal rights: The abolitionist approach.* Exempla Press.

[25] Francione, G. (2016, May 12). *Veganism as a moral imperative.* https://www.abolitionistapproach.com/veganism-moral-imperative

[26] Francione, G. (2021). *Why veganism matters: The moral value of animals.* Columbia University Press.

Eco Justice

[1] Australian Association of Social Workers (AASW). (2020). *Code of ethics.* AASW.

[2] Ryan, T. (2011). *Animals and social work: A moral introduction.* Palgrave Macmillan.

[3] Young, I. (1990). *Justice and the politics of difference.* Princeton University Press.

[4] Fraser, N. (2009). Who counts? Dilemmas of justice in post westphalian world. *Antipode, 41*(1), 281–297.

[5] Ross, D. (2020). *The revolutionary social worker love ethic companion.* Revolutionaries.

[6] United Nations (1948, December 10). *Universal declaration of human rights.* https://www.un.org/en/about-us/universal-declaration-of-human-rights

[7] United Nations (2006, December 12). *Convention on the rights of persons with disabilities.* https://www.ohchr.org/en/instruments-mechanisms/instruments/convention-rights-persons-disabilities

[8] United Nations (2007, September 13). *Declaration on the rights of Indigenous peoples.* https://www.un.org/

development/desa/indigenouspeoples/wp-content/
uploads/sites/19/2018/11/UNDRIP_E_web.pdf

9 Brueckner, M., & Ross, D. (2010). *Under corporate skies: A struggle between people, place and profit.* Fremantle Press.

9 Ross, D., & Puccio, V., (2020). Homegrown community activism in Yarloop. In D. Ross., M. Brueckner, M. Palmer & W. Eaglehawk (Eds.). *Eco-activism and social work: New directions in leadership and group work* (pp. 26–38). Routledge.

10 United Nations (n.d.). *Sustainable development goals.* https://sdgs.un.org/goals

11 United Nations (n.d.). *What is the Kyoto protocol?* https://unfccc.int/kyoto_protocol

12 Dorsch, P. (2022, October 24). *One in eight people in Australia are living in poverty.* Poverty & inequality. https://povertyandinequality.acoss.org.au poverty one-in-eight-people-in-australia-are-living-in-poverty

13 Ainsworth, K. (2023). *The cost of living has reached a record high, businesses are struggling, and interest rates are rising. Is a recession coming?* ABC News. https://www.abc.net.au/news/2023-05-03/record-high-living-costs-businesses-contracting-interest-rates/102296992

14 Eaglehawk, W. (2020). Species justice is for everybody. In D. Ross, M. Brueckner, M. Palmer & W. Eaglehawk (Eds.). *Eco-activism and social work: New directions in leadership and group work* (pp. 100–110). Routledge.

15 Francione, G. (2016, May 12). *Veganism as a moral imperative.* https://www.abolitionistapproach.com/veganism-moral-imperative

[16] Alger, K. (2020). *Five essays for freedom: A political primer for animal advocates*. Revolutionaries.

[17] Nagesh, A. (2017, December 31). *The harrowing psychological toll of slaughterhouse work*. Metro. https://metro.co.uk/2017/12/31/how-killing-animals-everyday-leaves-slaughterhouse-workers-traumatised-7175087/

[18] Singer, P. (2023). *Animal liberation now*. Jonathan Cape & BH - Trade.

[19] hooks, b. (2001). *Salvation: Black people and love*. William Morrow.

[20] Willett, C. (2014). *Interspecies ethics*. Columbia University Press.

[21] Worrall, S. (2015, July 15). *Yes, animals think and feel. Here's how we know*. National Geographic. https://www.nationalgeographic.com/animals/article/150714-animal-dog-thinking-feelings-brain-science

[22] White, R. (2009). Environmental victims and resistance to state crime through transnational activism. *Social Justice, 36*(3), 46–60.

[23] Frangoul, A. (2022, December 16). *Planned wind farm told it will have to shut down 5 months a year to protect parrots*. CNBC. https://www.cnbc.com/2022/12/16/wind-farm-will-need-to-shut-down-five-months-a-year-to-protect-parrots.html

[24] Poelina, A. (2020). First law is the natural law of the land. In D. Ross., M. Brueckner, M. Palmer & W. Eaglehawk (Eds.). *Eco-activism and social work: New directions in leadership and group work* (pp. viii–xii). Routledge.

[25] Thomashow, M. (2014, December 19). *What is the ecological imagination?* https://www.mitchellthomashow.com/blog/

what-is-the-ecological-imagination

[26] Higgins, P. (2010). *Eradicating ecocide: Laws and governance to prevent the destruction of our planet.* Shepheard-Walwyn Publishers.

[27] Wooltorton, S., Poelina, A., & Collard, L. (2021). River relationships: For the love of rivers. *River Research and Applications, 38*(3), 393–403.

[28] Youth Verdict (n.d.). *We're fighting for First Nations people to have sovereign decision-making power over traditional lands and lead action on climate change to ensure a future where we all thrive.* https://www.youthverdict.org.au/

[29] Toomey, J. (2022, November 25). *Queensland Land Court rules against Clive Palmer's Waratah coal mine in a landmark ruling.* ABC News. https://www.abc.net.au/news/2022-11-25/qld-court-waratah-coal-mine-youth-climate-activists-clive-palmer/101698906

[30] Jecks, D. (2020). Hands off Point Peron. In D. Ross, M. Brueckner, M. Palmer & W. Eaglehawk (Eds.), *Eco-activism and social work: New directions in leadership and group work* (pp. 89–99). Routledge.

[31] Ross, D., Brueckner, M., Palmer, M., & Eaglehawk, W. (Eds.), *Eco-activism and social work: New directions in leadership and group work.* Routledge.

[32] Yoorrook Justice Commission (2023). *It's time to tell your truth.* https://yoorrookjusticecommission.org.au/

[33] Animal Liberation Tasmania (2023). *Animal Liberation Tasmania.* https://animalliberationtas.org/

34 Howe, C. (2023, February 8). *Australian Brumby Alliance loses Supreme Court case to stop culling in Victoria's alpine national park.* ABC

News. https://www.abc.net.au/news/2023-02-08/
supreme-court-rejects-australia-brumby-alliance-petition-
culling/101945668

[35] Simard, S. (2022). *Finding the mother tree: Uncovering the wisdom and intelligence of the forest.* Penguin Books.

A Theory of Revolutionary Love

[1] Bulloch, S. (2023, May 6). Teen's plea before suicide: 'They won't help me'. *The Courier Mail*, 11.

[2] Abuelaish, I. (2012). *I shall not hate.* Bloomsbury.

[3] Boochani, B. (2019). *No friends but the mountain: Writing from Manus prison.* (O. Tofighian Trans). Picador Australia.

[4] Poelina, A. (2020). First law is the natural law of the land. In D. Ross., M. Brueckner, M. Palmer & W. Eaglehawk (Eds.). *Eco-activism and social work: New directions in leadership and group work* (pp. viii–xii). Routledge.

[5] Alger, K. (2020). *Five essays for freedom: A political primer for animal advocates.* Revolutionaries.

[6] Victorian Royal Commission (2021). *Royal commission into Victoria's mental health system. Final Report.* https://finalreport.rcvmhs.vic.gov.au/

[7] Simard, S. (2022). *Finding the mother tree: Uncovering the wisdom and intelligence of the forest.* Penguin Books.

[8] hooks, b. (2001). *All about love: New visions.* William Morrow.

Epilogue: Personal Essays

[1] Wall Kimmerer, R. (2013). *Braiding sweetgrass: Indigenous wisdom, scientific knowledge and the teachings of plants.*

Penguin Books.

2 Brandon, D. (1973). *Zen in the art of helping.* Arkana Penguin Books.

3 Ragg, N. (1977). *People not cases: A philosophical approach to social work.* Routledge.

4 Titmuss, R. (1970). *The gift relationship: From human blood to social policy.* Policy Press.

5 Brown, B. (2010, June). *The power of vulnerability.* [Video]. TED Conferences. https://www.ted.com/talks/ brene_brown_the_power_of_vulnerability

6 hooks, b. (1994). T*eaching to transgress: Education as the practice of freedom.* Routledge.

7 Freire, P. (1970). *Pedagogy of the oppressed.* Herder & Herder.

8 Smyth, J., & Hattam, R. (2001). *Intellectual as hustler: Researching against the grain of the market.* Flinders Institute for the Study of Teaching.

9 Slang, E. (n.d.). *The mythical white lions of South Africa. Wisdom From North.* https://wisdomfromnorth.com/ the-mythical-white-lions-of-south-africa/

10 Willett, C. (2014). *Interspecies ethics.* Columbia University Press.

11 For example, see Sandra Wooltorton's words in: Poelina, A., Wooltorton, S., Harben, S., Collard, L., Horwitz, P., & Palmer, D. (2020). *Feeling and hearing country.* PAN: Philosophy Activism Nature, 15, 6–15.

12 Alger, K. (2020). *Five essays for freedom: A political primer for animal advocates.* Revolutionaries.

13 Timeto, F. (2020). Becoming-with in a compost society – Haraway beyond posthumanism. *International Journal of Sociology and Social Policy, 41*(3/4), 315–330. https://doi.

org/10.1108/IJSSP-08-2019-0158

Postscript

[1] Mayo, T. (2023, October, 21-27). The right side of history. *The Saturday Paper*, 3.

www.ingramcontent.com/pod-product-compliance
Lightning Source LLC
Chambersburg PA
CBHW032122020426
42334CB00016B/1044